"A brilliant blend of science and soul. This is a book that the food world has needed for a long time." —FRED W. SAUCEMAN, author of *The Place Setting*

"Lundy invites you to sit at the table with a good hot biscuit and some buttery sorghum syrup and meet the people who grow it, make it, and even the chefs who have discovered it. For me and other people who grew up in the Appalachians, the stories offer a taste of home." —BELINDA ELLIS, author of *Biscuits*

"Infuses the sorghum artisan's pride into each recipe, providing a taste of cooking with heritage." —JAMES BAIER, executive secretary, National Sweet Sorghum Producers and Processors Association

"Everyone who appreciates the storied intersection of food and culture deserves to savor this book. The recipes are a combination of reliable favorites and brilliant innovations." —SHERI CASTLE, author of *The Southern Living Community Cookbook*

"Whether offering authentic hill country classics or twenty-first-century novelties, Lundy's recipes and meditations explore the full range of sorghum's flavorsome possibilities. She reveals the affinities of sorghum with New Mexico's red chiles and West Indian ginger, citrus, and cardamom, as well as its long-cherished harmony with cornbread, buttermilk, sweet potatoes, and bacon." —DAVID S. SHIELDS, author of *Southern Provisions*

"Lundy not only showcases the rich history of sorghum, she goes deeper, showing how much southern chefs truly value the history and traditions of where we come from." —TRAVIS MILTON, chef de cuisine, Comfort Restaurant, Richmond, Va.

"A brilliant blend of science and soul. This is a book that the food world has needed for a long time."—FRED W. SAUCEMAN, author of *The Place Setting*

"Lundy invites you to sit at the table with a good hot biscuit and some buttery sorghum syrup and meet the people who grow it, make it, and even the chefs who have discovered it. For me and other people who grew up in the Appalachians, the stories offer a taste of home."—BELINDA ELLIS, author of *Biscuits*

"Infuses the sorghum artisan's pride into each recipe, providing a taste of cooking with heritage."—JAMES BAIER, executive secretary, National Sweet Sorghum Producers and Processors Association

"Everyone who appreciates the storied intersection of food and culture deserves to savor this book. The recipes are a combination of reliable favorites and brilliant innovations."—SHERI CASTLE, author of *The Southern Living Community Cookbook*

"Whether offering authentic hill country classics or twenty-first-century novelties, Lundy's recipes and meditations explore the full range of sorghum's flavorsome possibilities. She reveals the affinities of sorghum with New Mexico's red chiles and West Indian ginger, citrus, and cardamom, as well as its long-cherished harmony with cornbread, buttermilk, sweet potatoes, and bacon."—DAVID S. SHIELDS, author of *Southern Provisions*

"Lundy not only showcases the rich history of sorghum, she goes deeper, showing how much southern chefs truly value the history and traditions of where we come from."—TRAVIS MILTON, chef de cuisine, Comfort Restaurant, Richmond, Va.

Sorghum's Savor

UNIVERSITY PRESS OF FLORIDA

Florida A&M University, Tallahassee
Florida Atlantic University, Boca Raton
Florida Gulf Coast University, Ft. Myers
Florida International University, Miami
Florida State University, Tallahassee
New College of Florida, Sarasota
University of Central Florida, Orlando
University of Florida, Gainesville
University of North Florida, Jacksonville
University of South Florida, Tampa
University of West Florida, Pensacola

Sorghum's Savor

RONNI LUNDY

University Press of Florida

Gainesville · Tallahassee · Tampa · Boca Raton

Pensacola · Orlando · Miami · Jacksonville · Ft. Myers · Sarasota

20 19 18 17 16 15   6 5 4 3 2 1

Library of Congress Control Number: 2014953609
ISBN 978-0-8130-6082-8

The University Press of Florida is the scholarly publishing agency for the State
University System of Florida, comprising Florida A&M University, Florida
Atlantic University, Florida Gulf Coast University, Florida International University,
Florida State University, New College of Florida, University of Central Florida,
University of Florida, University of North Florida, University of South Florida,
and University of West Florida.

University Press of Florida
15 Northwest 15th Street
Gainesville, FL 32611-2079
http://www.upf.com

Contents

Introduction

You dip your cane stalk down into the boiling
pan, catch the yellow foam on the end of the
stalk, wave it in the air until it's cooled down
some, and suck it off. Again and again you dip
it in, for once you start there's no stopping. . . .
The taste of it puts you in mind of fall winds and
wood smoke and dancing in the fields and games
played in the secret dark.

Jean Ritchie, writing about sweet sorghum syrup
in *Singing Family of the Cumberlands*

My memory is situated at the chrome dinette with the gray and
bright red laminate top. I am too little to reach it on my own in
one of the red vinyl chairs, and so I am cradled in a soft and ample
lap. Arms reach around me, heavy, crinkled, and tender. The hands
are rough, the skin cracked by years of working the garden, the
wash, the smoke house, the stove. Rough and cracked, but gentle
when they touch a child, and deft. They are working a fork in a
cool chunk of fresh butter, driving the tines down to smash and
separate, then moving back and forth to blend, and then driving
down again. When the butter is soft and malleable enough, the
hands put down the fork, pick up a big spoon and a Ball jar full
of dark, dark amber. The spoon goes in, and a thick dollop comes
out and oozes down on the butter. The fork begins to work it,

blended dark gold. A voice from behind me, soft and happy, sings, "Mmmm. Mmmm. Mmmm."

This is my great-aunt Johnnie, who delights in giving me little bites of any treat that it crosses her mind to share. Slivers of sharp, acid June apples as she cores and slices them to dry, sun-warmed Tommy Toes from the garden vines, pale gold–dripping honeycomb from Aunt Bert's hives. But this amber syrup is not honey; it's darker and its sweet fragrance also has a sharp tang.

Across the table my great-uncle Charlie sits, an expectant smile on his wide cat face. It may be my mama who delivers the hot biscuits to the table, or one of my other great-aunts. There's a scraping of the chairs as everyone settles in. Johnnie reaches out in front of me for a golden biscuit so hot she tosses it from one hand to the next before she breaks it open, breaks off a chunk of white steaming fluff and crust. She blows on it, over my head, and when it's cool enough to eat but still "good and warm," she lifts the fork with its shiny ochre bounty and wipes it into the biscuit's heart. "Open wide," she says, and pops it into my mouth.

The sensations are complicated, and I give them the total focus of a child. There's sweet, but with a plangent note that honey lacks. It's a sweet that reaches down into the throat, followed by just a little sour. It tastes of earth, and grass. There is the butter, of course, but in tandem with it the syrup has an unguent nature of its own. It fills my mouth in a way that sugar never has. It lingers. It beckons. I chew, swallow, and say, "More." Charlie's grin lights up like Christmas, Johnnie laughs, everyone around the table smiles, and my daddy says, "Give that baby some more 'lasses."

This is how folks feed babies in the mountains. This is how I first came to know sorghum's savor.

The table in this memory was in the kitchen of my great-aunts' house in Corbin, Kentucky, the southern Appalachian town where I was born. I grew up in Louisville, though, the Ohio Valley city where my family moved when I was about a year old so my father could find work. Like most members of the hillbilly diaspora, we never fully left the mountains. I spent large swatches of my summers with my cousins, uncles, and aunts; we went "up home" on long weekends, for reunions, and winter holidays. And when Daddy's work made it impossible for us to travel, the relatives would come to our house. When they did, they came bearing gifts of food, the taste of home.

Sorghum syrup was in the pantry or on the table all my early life, and for a long time I assumed that was so for everyone. My family, like most folks from our region, called this elixir "sorghum molasses" or just plain "molasses," or sometimes "'lasses," like my daddy did, when the tang of it "really hit the spot." When I left home in my early twenties and set up housekeeping in the mountains of the West, I assumed that bottle in the grocery with the label saying "molasses" contained the selfsame stuff. I bought some that first winter and wondered when I poured it on my butter and began to mash why it was such a dark, dark brown, almost black. And then the literally bitter truth: That molasses tasted nothing like my memory. Its sweet was flat, its aftertaste brackish and harsh, and there was no buttery resonance, no "please sir, I want some more."

I pushed my plate away and put the jar at the far back of the shelf, wondering if I had, as Thomas Jefferson was once accused, become someone who "abjured [my] native victuals." But a raid of my mother's pantry the next time I was there assured me I had not. The sorghum I spooned out in her kitchen still tasted succulent and full and complicated and fine. Eventually I learned that while sorghum syrup was called molasses, molasses it was not.

I also learned to buy a jar of the good stuff any time I came across one when I was in the southeastern part of the United States, where it seemed most prevalent in stores or in the roadside produce stands that dotted back roads. I put it on my biscuits and my sweet potatoes (sometimes with candied ginger crushed in). I mixed it with peanut butter for sandwiches, as country music icon Chet Atkins had told me he liked to do when he was growing up in east Tennessee. Sorghum was essential for such Appalachian sweets as stack cakes, gingerbread, and fried apple pies. It was the reason my baked beans were better than any others. But my compulsion to buy sorghum syrup anytime I saw it meant I sometimes had an assortment of three or four different jars. I learned that sorghum is the Zen sweetener: You never taste the same syrup twice. Like wine, the syrup's flavor varies from season to season, region to region, and from one boil to another.

That abundance, and the different possibilities of each jar, led me to experiment with a little sorghum in unlikely places. I put some in my burgoo for resonance and added a little to temper the hot and salty of my country ham jambalaya. I tried it in my New Mexico red enchilada sauce. It played well with garlic and tomatoes in marinara. It was, of course, a part of any barbecue sauce I made, but then it crept over into almost all my marinades. It was particularly nice when used with Asian foods, its full, rounded resonance leading me to call it "Hillbilly Umami."

I also started to wonder why the great chefs weren't all over this amazing ingredient. And then I discovered that some of them—most often those working in a southern vernacular—certainly were.

"Hey, did you hear Edward Lee on the radio today," a friend asked? "He was supposed to talk about his restaurant in Louisville and the Derby, but all he could do was go on about that sorghum stuff you like so much."

I found Charleston/Nashville restaurateur Sean Brock online waxing poetic about sorghum's intricate play of flavors, its force in creating community. I sat down to break bread with Ouita Michel at the Holly Hill Inn in Midway, Kentucky, and as she poured out some 'lasses, she was laughing, pouring out a story, too, about her eighty-plus-year-old sorghum-making neighbor, the indomitable Lucy Breathitt.

Turns out that just about every sorghum has a story, and every chef who knows this has a unique take on how to use it. And everybody—perhaps with a little drive and surely with a visit to the Internet—can nowadays find a source for the good stuff. And it seemed to me it was about time to give this amazing American ingredient a well-deserved shout out.

So here we go.

Matters of Definition

Sorghum molasses is what my family most often called the sweet syrup in our pantry, pronouncing it "sahr-gum" because we were mountain folks. Elsewhere it might come out more like "sore-gum" and occasionally the terse "ser-gum." If my mother just said, "Hand me that jar of molasses," I knew what she meant. She meant sorghum. But when I left her kitchen, things were not so simple. It turns out that the sweet syrup my family so loved has many names, and those names have potentially confusing definitions. So, a few words about words would be in order here.

Sorghum is an Old World grass. You may have driven past a field of sorghum taking it for corn, which it resembles visually. The majority of sorghum is cultivated to be used as a grain, primarily for feeding cattle, although in recent years as concern about gluten or wheat intolerance has increased along with curiosity about unusual grains, a very small portion of grain sorghum has been marketed for culinary purposes, too. Sorghum flour, with a pale beige color and slightly sweet taste, is available in specialty groceries, as are sorghum kernels to be used as popcorn.

Meanwhile, some varieties of this grass are known as sweet sorghum because they produce a large amount of sugar in their stalks. These varieties have been cultivated over the years not to be used for grain, but to have the cane juice extracted and processed to make sweet sorghum syrup. That syrup has been commonly referred to as sorghum molasses or simply molasses—a tendency

not only among consumers but also of many producers of sweet sorghum syrup.

Originally the seeds were marketed as a substitute for sugar cane, so further confusion stems from the fact that old-timers often called their sorghum cane simply "sugar cane." Still today you can meet folks who swear their daddy grew sugar cane at a latitude and altitude where it simply couldn't be done. They are referring in the old way to sweet sorghum cane, and they are equally apt to insist that what that cane produced was molasses.

But sweet sorghum syrup isn't technically true molasses. Molasses is a by-product of the refining process used to make sugar. Sugar is made by extracting the sweet juice from sugar cane or beetroots and boiling it multiple times until crystals form. The crystals are then removed with a centrifuge, leaving a syrupy run-off called molasses.

Beet molasses is not particularly palatable to people, so it is used as an additive in cattle feed. Sugar cane typically goes through three boiling cycles, the first producing a light molasses that is commonly called cane syrup. The second boil produces molasses and the third blackstrap molasses. With each boil, the molasses becomes decreasingly sweet and increasingly bitter until you reach blackstrap's almost medicinal flavor.

Sorghum doesn't easily lend itself to refining into crystals as sugar cane and beets do, so sweet sorghum is processed directly to produce syrup. The juice is crushed (or as old-timers like to say, "squeezed") from the cane and then heated until a thick, rich syrup results. That syrup is not the by-product of anything, but the whole point, hence sorghum syrup is not really molasses.

But try telling that to folks who've been eating sorghum molasses or sorghum by the name of molasses all their lives! The National Sweet Sorghum Producers and Processors Association, an organization that does an excellent job of describing itself in its own name, has tried. In an attempt to differentiate their pure product from run-off molasses and other lesser or adulterated syrups in the marketplace, the NSSPPA has encouraged members to market and refer to their product as "sorghum syrup" or "sweet sorghum syrup."

But when I interviewed Kentuckian Danny Townsend, one of the top commercial sweet sorghum syrup producers in the country, and a former president of the NSSPPA, he referred to the silky amber-colored liquid twice as "molasses" in the first five minutes of conversation. When he saw me poised to ask at the second mention, he grinned, "I know, I know. I try to call it sweet sorghum syrup, but a habit's a hard thing to break."

That's true, but from here on out, I'll put my habits aside and refer to this lovely elixir as sorghum syrup or just plain sorghum. If I need to talk about sorghum flour or sorghum kernels, that's what I'll call them.

But if you come to my house and ask for sugar in your coffee, I just may ask you if you might instead like to "try it with a little 'lasses."

"Long sweetening" was the term used in the southern mountains for sorghum syrup, while "short sweetening" meant store-bought sugar. I've heard a couple of theories why, including the reasoning that sorghum takes so long to drip off your spoon while sugar can plop into your coffee in no time flat. Appalachian food scholar Fred Sauceman, a sweet sorghum expert, told me that author Joe Dabney, another Appalachian food expert, suggested that sugar came by its name because it was so often in short supply, while sorghum was around for the long haul. I like to think that the terms arose because sugar is the very definition of instant gratification, here in a burst, gone in a second, but sorghum's taste lingers, lingers, lingers.

Long Sweeteners

OUITA MICHEL

Ouita Michel is a chef with many kitchens in central Kentucky. She keeps sorghum in every one.

She says, "We use a ton of sorghum at Woodford," meaning at Woodford Reserve Distillery in Versailles, Kentucky, where she is chef-in-residence, creating menus for special events. There they serve a sorghum mint julep and a signature vinaigrette with bourbon and sorghum. It's also in the brine for their pork loins and, she notes, "Sorghum just has so much affinity for bourbon. We keep coming up with recipes where it just clicks."

It clicks also in the spicy pecan pie she sometimes serves at Windy Corner, her casual country eatery off the Paris Pike in the bluegrass; in the locally made salty sorghum ice cream offered in pints at her Smithtown Seafood, in an urban neighborhood in Lexington; in the slaw served at Wallace Station, her deli in Versailles; and in the molasses cookies turned out of her Midway School Bakery in Midway, Kentucky, just up the road from Holly Hill Inn, where sorghum frequently dances with sweet potatoes.

That's a lot of use for an ingredient that Ouita admits she didn't initially hold in high regard. "I didn't think I liked sorghum because I don't like grocery store molasses, and I mistakenly thought they were the same. I owe my conversion to Lucy Breathitt," she laughs.

Lucy Breathitt is a delightful octogenarian widow from old bluegrass lineage. "Her family sold the first thoroughbred in the North Americas," Ouita explains. "Lucy was Nixon's social secretary and a lifelong Republican, but Governor Ned Breathitt [a prominent Kentucky Democrat] was her husband late in life.

"She drives a beat up farm truck with a 'Legalize Hemp' bumper sticker on it. The first time I met her, she got out of the truck with her dog, Mac, and said, 'Well. This is Mac. Mac Breathitt. He's a Republican.'

"I said, 'How do you know?'

"She said, 'Well. The first time he met Governor Breathitt, he peed all over his shoes.'"

From there a great friendship was born. Lucy grew pansies and violets that she supplied to Holly Hill for years. When she lost her tobacco base in the early 2000s, like several enterprising Kentucky farmers, she turned that acreage over to sorghum cane.

"She talked a contractor into building a sorghum house for her processing. She called hers Woodford Gold [after Woodford County] and we bought a ton of it," Ouita says. "We bought five-gallon buckets for the kitchen, but we also bought it in these little bottles that we'd put out on the table for brunch. I think I may still have some."

Ouita's eyes get that glowing, wistful look, like an oenophile remembering a once savored but now gone vintage. Lucy Brea-thitt got out of the sweet sorghum business a few years ago. Now Ouita's restaurants buy from other Kentucky producers including Country Rock in Versailles and Townsend's in Jeffersonville.

Her eyes start to spark again, "It's great to be in Kentucky because you can find consistently high-quality sorghum all the time, even if there are these subtle notes and changes from season to season from the same producer.

"Sorghum syrups are like bourbons. Each is different, and the more you sample, the more you start to understand what you like. Maybe five years ago I started to be able to discern the differences in different batches of sorghum. It's partly the process, but it's also the *terroir*. People don't think that's a real thing, but it definitely is. You can taste it. The limestone in this area comes through in the distinct minerality of central Kentucky sorghum. And when it's processed right, you can pick up the vegetal notes. It's a true expression of the farmer's soil condition. It's like a philosophy of sorghum."

Every Pitcher Tells a Story

As is often the case with ancient grains and foodstuffs, sorghum (*Sorghum bicolor [L.] Moench*) has a globe-trotting history that has both curious twists and mysterious gaps.

Sorghum is a tropical grass that most likely originated in Africa, traveled from there to Asia, and was cultivated in one or the other, or both, to become an edible grain. It spread to the Middle East and was used for centuries as flour, as a grain that could be cooked and eaten, or fermented for strong drink. It was also used as animal fodder. Broom sorghum was cultivated for its fibrous leaves, whose use gives its name. But where sweet sorghum comes in is still a bit of a mystery.

Sorghum seeds were part of the cargo of the slave ships that came to the Americas as early as the seventeenth century. It's presumed sorghum was brought to be used as a potential food for the enslaved, but as such it would have been most likely cultivated as a grain to be eaten as it was in Africa. In *Soul Food*, his study of African-American foodways, Adrian Miller notes that "West Africans didn't have dessert—a composed sweet course to end the sequence of an otherwise savory meal."

So as far as we know, sweet sorghum cane was not grown in the United States until the 1850s. That's when the variety known as Black Amber (sometimes called Chinese sugarcane) arrived by way of France and was distributed through the northern states, while imphee grass from South Africa made its appearance in the southern states.

Both "tropical" and "sugar cane" can be a bit misleading since sorghum cane can grow in far more temperate climates than actual sugar cane. Sorghum cane was introduced and cultivated for a while in Europe as a possible domestic replacement for imported sugar and syrup, although it didn't catch on.

But in the 1850s, when it arrived in North America, sweet

sorghum cane came with a complex political agenda, as well as an economic one. Conflict over slavery had northern states looking for an inexpensive source of sugar and sweetening that could be grown regionally and break dependence on, and the profits of, the sugar plantations of the South. Sweet sorghum cane looked likely. The cultivation and processing of Chinese sorghum began above the Mason-Dixon Line, primarily in the Midwest, and surged during the Civil War and for some time thereafter. Meanwhile, in South Carolina southern planters began experimenting with the South African seed. Historian David Shields notes that by 1857, twenty thousand acres of sweet sorghum were being grown from Minnesota to Georgia.

When the Civil War effectively destroyed the flow of sugar from Louisiana and Florida to the North in 1861, and after the Battle of Vicksburg in 1863, sorghum became the sweetener of choice across the divided nation.

Sorghum juice's chemical makeup differs from sugar cane's, however; it doesn't crystallize as easily. So while sorghum syrup became a readily available liquid sweetener, sorghum could not as easily replace granulated sugar. And the early methods of producing sorghum syrup were experimental, with sometimes dubious results. When the processor knew what he or she was doing, the outcome was a delicious sorghum syrup, but when not, the product could taste burned, sour, or brackish. So when southern cane sugar made its way back to the market after Reconstruction, and then when sugar beets were developed as a temperate climate source of sugar in the late 1800s, sorghum began to slowly lose favor as a sugar substitute. The cultivation of the sorghum plant gravitated back toward fodder, particularly in the West, where it became prized because of its drought resistance.

In the upper South, however, sweet sorghum had a second life. In the mountain South, particularly, it became a cash crop for some middle-class planters and a source of homegrown sweetening for poorer black, white, and American Indian families of the region. There is an ethic in the mountain South of doing for oneself, of not being "beholden." As such, homegrown sorghum syrup, in place of store-bought sugar, added to its already complex flavor profile a new element: the taste of independence.

The sweet, sticky substance also became the glue of community. Processing sorghum cane requires a mill for crushing the cane and extracting the juice and flat pans set over a steady fire for evaporating. Such equipment—particularly the mill—was beyond the purview of most subsistence or small farmers in the mountains and piedmont. In some communities there might be a single landowner with a mill for crushing, and folks would bring their cane to that place for a communal "squeezing" in the fall, mingling their crops into one sweet syrup that was then divided among them.

Jay Pierce, former executive chef at Lucky 32 in Greensboro, now at Rock Salt in Charlotte, North Carolina, and a major sorghum syrup fan, said that in addition to sorghum's being a great ingredient, its "alchemical aspect" is a primary attraction. "Sorghum is indicative of the way rural America used to be structured. For one of their primary needs, people had to come together. A sorghum boil is like a barn raising in that respect. You might have a field planted with the cane, and then you'd harvest it and bring it to your neighbor's. They'd have the mill and mule. And you'd put your cane in and it would be mingled with your neighbors,' and then the syrup would come out and it would be divided again among the people there, but altogether as one sorghum."

In *Foxfire 9*, blacksmith and wagon maker Jud Nelson of Sugar Valley, Georgia, recalled the mills of his childhood in the early part of the twentieth century: "Back then there was more syrup mills than there was blacksmiths, 'cause everybody had from a half acre to a' acre of syrup cane. Maybe one mill [to crush the cane] would be sittin' in one section and maybe eight miles on, someone else would have another one. They were just scattered around and people shared them. Usually the mill would be mounted on a wagon so they could take it around."

As Jud Nelson notes, in many rural communities the mill came to the sorghum instead of the other way around. Itinerant millers would roll their equipment up next to a field of cane and unhitch the mule or horse to turn the grinding wheel.

Danny Townsend, whose small, modernized operation in Jeffersonville, Kentucky, makes him one of the primary commercial sweet sorghum syrup producers in the country today, remembers that was still common in his youth. He recalls the roving miller also had a boiler: "He had furnaces on a rocker, made them easier to move. He'd set up next to the field, near the edge of a creek, give him water to temper the boiling and in case there was a fire. He'd cut right into the bank to make a firebox."

The process was still community oriented as neighbors would come to harvest and strip the cane, taking away jugs of sorghum as thanks and payment. The miller was usually paid in sorghum syrup—one gallon to every four was the going rate Jud Nelson recalled.

In her autobiography, *Singing Family of the Cumberlands*, folksinger Jean Ritchie called up the interwoven dark and light magic of sorghum and its making. Recalling a squeezing near Viper, Kentucky, in the mid-1930s, she wrote:

> The sky darkened and the hoot owls began to holler along the black ridges. If you looked away from the fire, up through the woods to the deep, deep gray sky and the cold pale stars, and heard the owls and other night birds singing their doleful songs, why then it seemed like a mighty scary, lonesome place to be in. Then you looked back quick at the bright blazing fire and the sweet molasses bubbling soft green-yellow bubbles in the big pan, and the boys and girls laughing and chasing one another, and lantern lights along the high hill

road bringing more and more folks to the party. That was a beautiful sight, and the warm brightness of it folded around you and kept you from the dark.

Sweet sorghum syrup (mixed with butter, or not) was spread on biscuits and cornbread. It was the focal ingredient in taffy pulls, popular house parties where young people would get together to make candy and eyes at one another back in earlier times. Sorghum gave humble mountain desserts like apple stack cake or gingerbread a buttery, haunting resonance. It was stirred into coffee, hot cereal, and cold milk. It put the flap in flapjacks, and for some artisan curers of hams or bacon, it was the secret ingredient that gave their pork a subtle boost of flavor.

In the mountains, sorghum was used in home remedies. A pinch of sulfur in a spoonful of sorghum followed by a big glass of water was used as a blood tonic, or to ward off flu; a pinch of soda in it to cure a cough; and for a sore throat you could simmer onions in it to make a soothing syrup. Fred Sauceman notes that patent medicines of the late 1800s and early 1900s frequently had sorghum syrup as an ingredient, and he has been told that some doctors would prescribe it for certain ailments.

It also sometimes led a secret double life.

Sorghum was often used to make moonshine. It grew more quickly and was less trouble than corn. A distiller could grow his own sweetening without calling much attention as buying big bags of sugar at the store surely would. During Prohibition and the Depression, sorghum's use in making spirits spread well beyond the mountain South, and there was a spike in sweet sorghum production nationally around this time.

Sucrat was one name given to sorghum rum that was home distilled up until the 1930s. Sorghum rum appears to be taking off again these days—but legally—as several regional artisanal distillers have been making their own versions. Colglazier and Hobson

Distilling Company out of Indianapolis claims their Sorgrhum (both dark and light) as the first and has a charming video on their website showing the process from field to mill to still to bottle. Other distillers making sorghum rum include Wilderness Trace (Harvest Rum) in Danville, Kentucky; Petzold Distilleries (Carl's Carolina Spiced Sorghum Rum) in Marshall, North Carolina; and Mississippi River Distilling Company (Dry Dock Sorgrhum) in Le Claire, Iowa.

(Beer has also traditionally been brewed with sorghum grain in Africa and Asia, and that is catching on in the United States as well, as brewers—both home and commercial—look for gluten-free substitutes. But the malted syrup sold for that purpose is made from sorghum grain, not sweet sorghum syrup from the juice of the cane.)

Sorghum rum may become more prevalent, as it has appeal in addition to its distinctive, subtly complex flavor. Sorghum is a naturally pest-resistant crop so that insecticides are not often used in its cultivation, giving it a more "natural" profile. And sorghum can be grown locally, providing support for small farms in the region. Wilderness Trace uses Danny Townsend's sorghum syrup, which is made about seventy miles from the distillery. And Matt Colglazier's story about the inception of Sorgrhum notes that the nearby Amish farmer he buys syrup from was just about to give up the old tradition before this new market came along.

New culinary interest has given sweet sorghum producers hope for an increasingly healthy future market as well. As fascination with southern food and foodways has grown over the last decade, sorghum syrup has had an increasing presence in restaurant kitchens. And the more adventurous chefs have discovered that the syrup's complex harmonies make it a stellar addition in the world's cuisines.

So sweet sorghum syrup continues to flow, 'round the world and back again.

Long Sweeteners

RONA ROBERTS

Rona Roberts loves Kentucky sweet sorghum syrup so much she decided to write a book about it. *Sweet, Sweet Sorghum: Kentucky's Golden Wonder* came out in 2011, an extension of Rona's local food website, www.savoringkentucky.com.

Kentucky's long tradition of sorghum syrup making has been growing exponentially in recent years, and Rona's website is a great place to read about the latest producer or event. She and her husband and business partner, Steve Kay, host a regular Monday night cornbread supper at their Lexington, Kentucky, house, and she says, "You can be sure a pitcher of sorghum is always on the table."

When the ebullient woman with short white hair and a huge, huge grin comes to meet me at a Lexington coffee shop, she brings a brown paper sack with a couple of jars to share, one a pint of prized early, super sweet Sugar Drip from Randall Rock's Country Rock sorghum.

"I can't imagine a day in my parents,' my grandparents,' or my great-grandparents' lives when there wasn't sorghum on the table," she recalls. Rona grew up in the country in Wayne County, a few miles outside of Monticello, Kentucky. "We didn't make dessert. Our something sweet to finish was sorghum on a biscuit or cornbread.

"My dad's dad made sorghum every year. In the community there was one guy with the mill, Mr. Gregory. He would come with his cooking pan and mill. The farmer had to provide the mule. Mr. Gregory got half of the sorghum that was made, and he sold it.

"My grandfather grew eight large stands. I'd say that provided a quarter cup a day for a year for everybody in the house. There were seven children and two adults, but there were always extra people—cousins, friends.

"My dad grew sorghum and probably only cooked it twice, but

that made such an impression on me. I loved it! We were running around wild all that day, no nap. My cousins all came. My cousins and I took the cane to dip in the foam and eat it. It stands out in my memory as a glory."

Like me, Rona grew up taking the availability of sorghum syrup for granted. But a few years ago, she began to notice it was harder and harder to find. Groceries stopped carrying it; it seemed as if the older makers were dying off and younger ones weren't replacing them. "I began to worry it was going to disappear from the world," she says. "*Sweet, Sweet Sorghum*, the impetus to write that book, came out of longing."

She says that before she even began work on the book, "I decided there'd be no mule in it. Whenever people write about sorghum syrup, seems like there's always a picture of a mule and the story's about the past. But I wanted to make the point, sorghum has a future!"

She's been heartened to see the product's resurgence in recent years, to note the affection of chefs who "discover" it. She notes with some pride that Good Foods Market in Lexington now carries it year round. But we talk about the difficulty of tracking it down for folks who live in regions without a strong tradition.

"You know, Morris Bitzer [the late University of Kentucky agricultural extension specialist whose contemporary studies of sorghum were extensive and significant], told me that at one time sweet sorghum was grown in all fifty contiguous states, so it shouldn't just be the southern mountains and piedmont that should have this heritage," she notes.

"But maybe it's not a bad thing that folks don't know a lot about it yet, that it takes some work to figure out how to get it. I think it adds to the mystique.

"What we have to do is encourage people to enter the mystery."

Big Wheels Keep on Turning

Although some of the machinery may have changed a bit, sweet sorghum syrup is essentially made today the same way it was in the 1850s.

The first step is the planting of the cane in the spring or late summer. There are a handful of varieties of sweet sorghum, each with slightly different characteristics, including sugar content in the cane, adaptability to climate and soil, pest resistance, and ripening times. Most producers figure out which they prefer, balancing ease of cultivation with the end product. (And it's worth noting that Mark Guenther, of Muddy Pond Sorghum Mill, one of the largest commercial producers in the country of sweet sorghum syrup, still uses mules to cultivate at the family's farm in Muddy Pond, Tennessee. Mark says it's not for nostalgia's sake but because he believes the mules are more sensitive to the plant and field, and hence do a better job.)

As the cane grows and ripens, the sugar content in its stalk increases up to a point, but then the sugar can begin to turn starchy, which results in a poorer quality syrup. Judging the optimum time to cut cane is part science and part art. Some producers take cues from the maturity level of seeds. Some use a Brix hydrometer or sugar refractor to measure the sugar content in the juice. Some taste. Ultimately the decision is made much as a vintner judges his or her grapes. The cane must be harvested before a hard freeze, however, as that will ruin the juice for syrup.

The stalks are deheaded and seed is often saved. Traditionally the cane was stripped of its leaves in the field by friends and/or hired workers, and then cut. Nowadays stripping is likely to be done mechanically, or some producers simply leave the leaves on. When they are removed, the leaves are commonly used for fodder or turned back into the soil as compost.

The cane is gathered and may be allowed to sit for a couple of days to lose some water, which makes the processing quicker. But the cane can't sit too long or the sugar content will begin to drop. Cut cane that is left too long may begin to rot at the cut end, as well, tainting the quality and flavor of the juice.

Mills are still relatively small, even at the more commercial operations, with a series of geared wheels and rollers that crush the cane to extract the juice. In the old days, those wheels were powered by a mule or a horse attached to a long pole (the sweep) that stretched across the top of the mill. As the animal took a step forward, the part of the pole behind him would be pulled toward him and the part of the pole in front would move away, keeping him in perpetual motion. The gears attached to the pole would turn the rollers to crush the cane. These days power comes from gasoline or electric motors, or sometimes by way of a belt hooked up to a tractor engine. Juice is strained as it comes out to get rid of fragments of stalk or the like. Modern operations allow the juice to "settle" in tanks for a short period (a half hour to three hours)

before processing. Some processors may preheat the juice in the settling tanks.

The juice is then heated to syrup stage in an open evaporating pan. Some operations still use wood fire, as in olden days, but most use gas, either for an open flame or steam heat. Evaporation needs to happen as quickly as possible, but not so quickly that the syrup burns. Also, heat must gradually increase as the syrup moves through the pan and coagulates. Controlling the heat becomes another skillful piece in the art of sorghum syrup production.

As the juice warms, proteins and other coagulants not wanted in the syrup rise to the top and must be skimmed off, usually with a perforated paddle that catches the scum but lets the pure juice flow through and back into the pan. Skimmings can be fed

to cattle later, since they are high in protein, or discarded. This evaporating and skimming process takes hours.

The evaporating pan is channeled and raised at the exit end. As juice is poured in and heats, it's moved slowly upward through the channels until it reaches the right color and consistency. Every sorghum producer I spoke with said that while there are methods now to judge the sugar content and instruments to fine-tune the heat and the process, making that call on when the syrup is ready is still the greatest matter of art.

The finished sorghum syrup is cooled and then decanted into containers to be put by for family and friends or sold.

Long Sweeteners

Doug Harrell

The morning has barely started but Doug Harrell greets us with strong coffee, hot biscuits, and butter with sweet sorghum syrup. He and his wife, Barbara, both approaching seventy, live in a house that's been in the Harrell family for six generations. The western North Carolina mountain farm it occupies outside of Bakersville was an original land grant in 1796. Doug and Barbara moved back to the land where he grew up in 1990, after living and working many years in Burlington.

"This is our sixth year doing sorghum," Doug says. When he was growing up, the farm was a dairy and burley tobacco operation. Doug and Barbara first tried growing and selling Christmas trees, "but so did everyone else in the area, so there was an oversupply. And the deer probably cost us half a million," he laughs.

Thinking of what could make a viable living, Doug said he realized, "It has to be something that has a high enough threshold of expense getting in or there's too much competition for the market to be profitable."

Because it requires investment in equipment, sorghum processing fit that profile, but with an added benefit for the Harrells. Because theirs had been a dairy farm, the Harrells were able to repurpose some of the equipment they'd been left with, something many sorghum producers do.

And Barbara notes that even though sorghum making has been prevalent in the region for generations, "the competition for making it is limited now because a lot of the people who did it have aged out."

"It's physically hard work at harvest and boiling time," Doug notes with a shake of his head. "When we boil, I'm at the barn at two in the morning and go until nine at night. The next morning, I'm up early to clean the pans."

That kind of work produced five hundred to six hundred gallons in the fall of 2012, which Doug sold in five Ingles supermarkets in the area, some convenience stores, and at the local chamber of commerce. When we meet, in early summer 2013, he has only three pints left, but he nevertheless insists on giving one to me and one to my friend.

Doug says they do a "farm day" every year where anyone can come watch the boil. As we walk up to the shed where they process, I note there are a couple of mules grazing on the sharp slope behind. I ask if he uses them to turn the mill, but Doug laughs and says, "No, they keep away coyotes." His mills date back to the early 1900s, he says, but they run on gas.

Doug says, "The raw juice should have a sugar content of 18 percent. Now with the old-timers, they'd just break the cane and taste it, but I use a gauge that measures." "Brix" is the term used for measuring sugar content in the syrup itself, and the measurement needs to be at least 74 to make sorghum syrup. Doug says, "We usually cook ours to 82. Less and it comes out thinner. If you turn a jar of sorghum over and it moves real quick, then you know the sugar content is a little low. A higher Brix also means there's more tang to the taste."

That tang in the taste is what sorghum cognoscenti look for, as do those who grew up on it. "The color's not so much an indicator of flavor as it is of the potash in the soil," Doug says, "but a darker color is often what old-timers look for because it's how they remember it. And we put the word 'molasses' on our label, sorghum molasses, because that's what folks around here grew up calling it."

Autumn Is Festival Time

There are many opportunities every fall to see and sample sorghum syrup turned out the old way. Some communities in sorghum-producing regions have multiday festivals with all the small-town trimmings, including demonstrations with mule- or horse-driven mills and open-fire evaporating.

Living museums that focus on mid-to-late-1800s pioneer life frequently schedule a sorghum boil as part of a fall festival. And many of the larger commercial producers will have an open house at their farms, where you may have the opportunity to compare and contrast old-style and new side by side. When I began to ask around the western North Carolina mountain region and piedmont, I was also told of smaller, more intimate events where family and friends were invited to participate, and I was often invited to attend.

What follows is a partial list of contemporary festivals or demonstrations. It is by no means comprehensive; check with your local farmers market or convention center to discover if there are any in your region. Also, things change, so be sure to use the contact information here to confirm an event is still scheduled before making plans.

ALABAMA

Shelby Iron Works Park's Fall Festival, Shelby, AL: About an hour south of Birmingham, the small town of Shelby is the site of a historic southern iron works. The annual mid-October festival features traditional sorghum processing and local foods including butterbeans, turnip greens, and boiled peanuts. Find out more at www.shelbyironworks.com.

ARKANSAS

Cane Hill Harvest Festival, Cane Hill, AR: This tiny town in the Ozarks celebrates the source of its name with sorghum squeezing, apple-butter making, and other events at the former Cane Hill College, now a regional museum. The festival is the third weekend in September. Find out more at www.ozarkmerchants.com/canehill_festival.html.

Heritage House Museum Sorghum Squeezin', Mount Ida, AR: At this early November event, both a mule-powered and tractor-powered mill are used to crush the cane. Mount Ida is called the Quartz Capital of the World, so who knows what magical mineral properties syrup from here might have! Find out more at www.hhmmc.org.

GEORGIA

Blairsville Sorghum Festival, Blairsville, GA: A part of this north Georgia community for more than forty years, the festival usually takes place over two weekends in mid-October and also includes live music, contests, arts, crafts, and food. Find out more at www.blairsvillesorghumfestival.com.

INDIANA

Crawford County Sorghum Festival, Marengo, IN: This mid-October event is held at the Crawford County High School, but folks who attend the festival are invited to visit the nearby Bye Family Sorghum Mill, where they can watch Charlie Bye, a fourth-generation sorghum maker, ply his trade. Find out more at www.crawfordcountyindiana.com/attractions/events-festivals/sorghum-festival.

IOWA

Old Threshers Reunion, Mt. Pleasant, IA: Mt. Pleasant hosts the Old Threshers Reunion at the end of August and start of September. Members of the Maasdam family, of Maasdam's Famous Home Made Sorghum of Lynnville, Iowa, often demonstrate there. Maasdam is one of the largest producers of sweet sorghum syrup outside the South, and you can find information at their website, www.maasdamsorghum.com. Information about the festival is at www.oldthreshers.org.

KENTUCKY

Morgan County Sorghum Festival, West Liberty, KY: This area of Kentucky's Appalachians has a continuing history of fine sorghum making. It's been celebrated at this annual festival in late September for almost fifty years. Find out more at www.morgancounty sorghumfestival.com.

MISSOURI

Sand Hill Sorghum Festival, Scotland County, MO: Tucked in a corner of northeastern Missouri, this intentional community practices organic and sustainable agriculture, producing a small number of items for sale, including honey and sweet sorghum syrup. Their annual harvest festival the last weekend of September is an opportunity to watch their sorghum being made, and if you are genuinely serious about it, there are sometimes opportunities to stay at the farm and participate in the harvest. Find out more at www.sandhillfarm.org.

NORTH CAROLINA

Old School Sorghum Festival, McDaniels Crossroads, NC: This mid-September festival takes place at the site of a former community school, which educated local children from 1924 to 1949. The building now houses a personal collection of artifacts open to the public once a year during the festival, which also features old-time sorghum making. Find out more at www.oldschoolsorghum.com.

OHIO

John R. Simon's Sorghum Festival, West Portsmouth, OH: John R. Simon wrote the book on *Cowboy Copas and the Golden Age of Country Music* and he also cooks up a fine batch of sorghum every autumn at the festival on his farm in the edge of the Appalachians. Find out more at www.sorghumbysimon.com.

OKLAHOMA

Wewoka Sorghum Festival, Wewoka, OK: Demonstrations are held at the Seminole Nation Museum, and in addition to sorghum making, include tool and soap making and American Indian foodways. The festival occurs in late October. Find out more at www.seminolenationmuseum.org/events/sorghum-festival.

TENNESSEE

The Museum of Appalachia's Tennessee Fall Homecoming, Clinton, TN: This living museum has an annual celebration of southern mountain heritage every October. The folks from nearby Muddy Pond Sorghum Mill are part of a multifaceted menu of Appalachian arts and crafts. Find out more at www.museumof appalachia.org/events-upcoming.

Muddy Pond Sorghum Mill, various locations in TN: In addition to participating in the Museum of Appalachia's event, Muddy Pond does multiple demonstrations throughout Tennessee, from Dollywood to Cades Cove in Smoky Mountain National Park. For a current list of appearances, see www.muddypondsorghum.com/Festivals.html.

TEXAS

Labor Day Sorghum Festival, Brazos de Dios, TX: Homestead Heritage is a religious community located five miles north of Waco. The group's year-round Traditional Craft Village, open daily except Sunday, is the site of the annual Sorghum Festival on Labor Day Monday. Find out more at www.heritageministries.net/annualevents.html.

VIRGINIA

White Top Mountain Sorghum Molasses Festival, Independence, VA: Mount Rogers, the tallest peak in Virginia, is just west of Independence, and this is where the local fire department boils down sorghum and cooks up apple butter every year to raise money. Find out more at www.mtrogersvfd-rs.com.

VARIOUS LOCATIONS

The National Sweet Sorghum Producers and Processors Association maintains an events page that lists additional festivals annually. In recent years, Wisconsin has had several events at which Richard Wittgreve of Rolling Meadows Sorghum Mill appeared. Find out more at nssppa.org/Events_Calendar.html.

Long Sweeteners

DANNY TOWNSEND

"You could say I been marked by sorghum," Kentuckian Danny Townsend grins. "I've been around sorghum molasses all my life. Got the scars to prove it. I like to got my foot burned off when I was three years old, running barefoot over the coals of my grandpa's boiling fire."

Those aren't his only battle scars. Danny's family has been making sorghum syrup for five generations. He has a tempered fondness for tradition. When he does demonstrations, like his annual gig at the town of Mount Sterling's Court Days, he uses a mule to turn the wheel for squeezing and cooks his sorghum in a long open pan over a wood fire. It's a process that requires constant skimming.

I notice that every time Danny says the word "skimming" he rubs his left shoulder. He grins again. "I blew my shoulder out from that skimming." That's why he figured out a new process to eliminate as much of the skimming as possible.

Danny's is one of the larger commercial sorghum syrup operations in the country, which doesn't mean it's large in any kind of industrial sense, but it is modernized. On his Jeffersonville, Kentucky, farm, the sorghum cane is juiced using a motor, not a mule. Danny does his processing in a high-ceilinged frame outbuilding the size of a large barn. There's a long channeled open pan I recognize as the evaporator pan, but just beyond it is a second smaller but similar pan. And in the middle of the space are shining raised kettles.

continued

Danny explains that he preheats his sorghum juice in the kettles. As the juice heats, the sediment falls to the bottom and the "scum" rises to the top, just as it does when it's processed straight in the evaporator pans. But instead of having to skim the scum by hand (and arm and shoulder) the old-fashioned way, Danny drains the syrup from spigots a few inches above the bottom of the kettle. "After it's heated we drain the syrup out of here and turn it off before the scum comes out. The bulk of the scum stays right there in the kettle. Saves your shoulder plenty."

From there the syrup goes into the first channeled evaporator pan. It's heated by steam pipes below to cook and thicken it. When it's heated to the right consistency, the point where most operations start draining it off directly into tubs and jars, Danny instead drains it into the second, smaller channeled pan. This one has pipes underneath, too, but filled with cold water, so the syrup cools some before he bottles it.

"That gives me a lot more control over flavor," Danny says, noting that when the syrup is bottled hot without the cooling-pan step, it continues to cook a bit in the jar, to thicken and darken some from the residual heat.

While we talk, a young married couple from the Homestead Heritage Community outside of Waco, Texas, arrives. Homestead is a religious community where pioneer handcrafts are still practiced and many products, including their sorghum syrup, are sold in a store on-site and over the Internet. At Homestead Heritage they grind their organic cane using two mules to power the mill, and they heat in open copper pans.

Joel and Crissa Lancaster say that a growing increase in sales of the syrup have sent them cross-country to look at other methods of processing, and that "Danny Townsend is the man" they have heard they need to speak with.

The three talk for a bit about using the cane for compost and about the future possibilities of using the sugar to make plastic bottles, carpet, or even rubber for tires. They discuss the current research into using sorghum as a source of ethanol, noting that it grows faster and with less upkeep than corn. Danny says, "I'm not looking to fuel the world, just want to run the machinery on my farm."

They talk varieties of sorghum, and Joel says, "We grow three acres of Dale, that's all we've ever done."

"Hey, if it works," Danny nods, then he laughs. "Daddy like to run me off the farm when I started with Dale. See, two varieties of sorghum don't cook the same way in the pan. He come in the day after we first boiled that Dale and you couldn't stick a chisel in that syrup. We learned how to cook it, though."

I ask how, and he shakes his head at such a foolish question, then demonstrates:

"You get you a pan (he points at the evaporator pan).

"You get you a plate (he mimes holding a plate).

"You eat what comes off that pan (lifts imagined spoon to mouth and winces, does it again and grins).

"You'll learn how to do it right quick."

Come and Get It!

At the time that I was taking my first taste, most sweet sorghum syrup was still being produced the old-fashioned way, with a horse or mule to drive the mill that ground the cane, with syrup boiled in open pans over outdoor wood fires. My family usually knew or were related to someone "up in the country" who they bought syrup directly from, although you could find it for sale in country stores and cider stands in rural areas and in the produce markets in some towns or cities with strong rural roots. Until I left Kentucky and discovered its absence elsewhere, I took my easy access to sweet sorghum syrup for granted.

Once I learned, I became a bit of an acquisitive hoarder, buying a jar anytime I saw some. That meant that a trip to the Western North Carolina Farmers Market in Asheville, or the Kentucky State Fair, or Paul's Produce in Louisville might find me with three to four jars from different makers in my reusable grocery sack. I started giving them to friends in far-flung places like Maine or New Mexico, and when they'd run out and ask me where they could get some more, I often had to say they'd need to wait until I passed that way again.

And then the wide world's web of Internet commerce began. Now sweet sorghum syrup is just a Google away. And while it is still most extensively grown and marketed in the southeastern states (Kentucky and Tennessee lead in production), it can be found as well in Oklahoma, Texas, Kansas, Illinois, Ohio, Iowa, Minnesota, with more producers cropping up regularly.

But while you can order sweet sorghum syrup fairly easily on-line, and that's a great way to get to know the subtle differences in flavor from one *terroir* to another, there are always good reasons to seek out and support a producer close to home, if possible.

One very important reason is that knowing the integrity of the maker is the best way to know the integrity of the product.

Sweet sorghum syrup is not so diligently regulated—nor even uniform—in regard to labeling. So it's likely that the jar saying "Sorghum Molasses" that you find for sale may, indeed, be filled with 100 percent sweet sorghum syrup. But it could be sorghum syrup and sugar molasses mixed. And occasionally it may be sorghum syrup cut with corn syrup to reduce the chance of crystallization and "extend" it. Technically, if other ingredients are present, the label should say so somewhere in the fine print. But with so much good sorghum being made by small mom-and-pop operations, and a little bit being distributed that is not, that doesn't always happen.

To help consumers and producers alike, the National Sweet Sorghum Producers and Processors Association has created a logo for members to use as a label on jars and on websites and promotional material. The label indicates that the member has complied with association guidelines and that the product they are selling is unadulterated pure sweet sorghum syrup. In addition, the association maintains a website at nssppa.org and there keeps a list of active members from whom consumers can purchase sweet sorghum syrup, along with the sellers' contact information.

But not all sweet sorghum syrup producers are members of the NSSPPA, and not all members put the logo on their product or are listed on the website. You may find a promising-looking sorghum syrup being sold at a small country store with a label that lacks the logo. That doesn't mean it's not the real thing. But it's a good time to ask the merchant what she knows about where the sorghum comes from. If the store's owner tells you about a family up the road that's been making sorghum for a couple of generations, buy that jar. In fact, buy two. If the label tells you the name of the producer/processor (not a distributor) and identifies a location or phone where you might contact them, that's a good sign, too.

But if the merchant tells you it comes from a distributor not from around there, well, you might be just a little more cautious. It could be a fine, pure sorghum, or it might not. If the distributor has a phone number, it's worth a call to ask where their sorghum is coming from. If they can't or won't tell you specific makers and where they are located, you may want to pass.

And say you don't drive past that many roadside sorghum stands or country stores on your way to work. You may need to do a little sleuthing. A great place to start is at the nearest farmers market. You may find sorghum being sold there in the fall, but even if you don't, ask some of the vendor farmers if they know of someone in the region who still makes it.

State or county fairs are another likely place. Most have extensive agricultural exhibits where sorghum makers may be sampling and selling wares. You can check with your county's agricultural extension agent, also. He or she will likely have a finger on the pulse of what's happening. And Rona Roberts, author of *Sweet, Sweet Sorghum: Kentucky's Golden Wonder*, suggests you visit some local feed stores in the nearest agricultural region. "One way to find out if someone is producing in your area is to just go in and ask who's bought sweet sorghum seeds," Rona says.

To be sure you're getting good, pure sorghum syrup when ordering from the Internet, you can also refer to the NSSPPA list for confirmation that your source is legitimate or use the same sorts of judgment if not listed there. In many cases a website will belong to a family or community (some Amish, Mennonite, or other spiritual or intentional communities make and sell sweet sorghum syrup). The website may tell you all you need to know about their process and product so you can order with confidence. If you are ordering from a general store online, it never hurts to write or call and ask about their sources.

Why does it matter? Sorghum syrup is more difficult to produce than either corn syrup or molasses, making it a more expensive commodity. You want to be sure you get what you pay for.

Sweet sorghum cane is a non-GMO (genetically modified organism) crop. Corn syrup may have been made with GMO corn, and that matters to many consumers. Additionally, sorghum can usually be raised with minimal pesticide use, particularly compared to corn.

But most important are the differences in sensory quality, particularly fragrance and flavor. Molasses has a harsher taste than sorghum, more bitter, less sweet, and definitely less complex. Corn syrup has a bland, one-dimensional taste that fades from the mouth almost immediately. It will not linger, one of sorghum's most attractive aspects. Corn syrup and molasses are also not as sweet as sorghum, so syrups that are blended will not deliver on that count. (To clarify, high-fructose corn syrup is corn syrup that has undergone enzymatic processing to convert some of its glucose to fructose and intensify its sweetness. The corn syrup that is occasionally used to dilute sorghum syrup is almost always regular corn syrup, not high fructose.)

Incidences of deceit in the marketing of sorghum syrup are relatively small, but seeking out a reputable producer is the best way to ensure you are getting the genuine sweet sorghum syrup and so is worth the effort.

Long Sweeteners

EDWARD LEE

When New York City chef Edward Lee decided to set up shop in Louisville, Kentucky, he bought Eddie Garber's 610 Magnolia lock, stock, and pantry.

"Ten years ago the whole southern revival thing was not really happening yet," Edward recalls. "In Eddie Garber's time it was fancy food, Euro-centric, so I inherited shelves of honey from Provence, maple syrup from Vermont."

And that's what he was using in dishes until one afternoon, riding his motorcycle on a back road in southern Indiana, he passed a roadside stand. There were jars of something on it, so he turned back to see what that was.

"They were jars that said 'sorghum.' I knew it originated in Africa, so I asked the guy, 'Is this from Africa?' and he's like, 'No, man, its from forty minutes down the road.'"

As a chef, Edward Lee has made his name over the last ten years extrapolating on the serendipity of combining his food heritage—Korean cuisine—and the products and repertoire of his newly and passionately adopted southern home. But he says, "I'm not going to buy local just for the sake of local. That sorghum, though, it met every criterion I look for!

"It has more depth and range than honey, a more complex umami. And I thought, 'Why am I using a sweetener from a thousand miles away when this is right up the road?

"I bought a whole box filled with sorghum jars and I told my cooks, throw out the honey we have and just use this."

Edward says he did eventually decide that honey has its place "just for very, very delicate food, and mostly on the sweet side. It's best really as a finishing perfume. Sorghum I use for anything savory and for the more unctuous desserts.

"One of the first dishes I used it in was a foie gras. We'd been doing it with honey, but sorghum was so much better. It was able to stand toe-to-toe with foie gras. It has so much structure. We painted the plate with sorghum, served both seared and cold foie gras with different garnishes: a little fresh jalapeno, popped sorghum seeds, toasted farro, herbs like tarragon, chervil, something anise, nothing too aromatic."

He says, "We haven't yet explored all of sorghum's permutations [as an ingredient]. I love using sorghum syrup with smoky flavors, anything with burned or caramelized flavors, anything over an open fire. It's the harmony.

"It also works as counterpoint. Anise works because it's so different. And because [sorghum is] nuttier and richer than any other syrup, it works with brown butter."

He's been consulting with Danny Townsend recently to try a lighter cooking time "to see how blond we can go. Why? If you've ever tasted the raw juice—it's delicious! I'm curious to see if we can capture that. Everyone's told me that if we don't cook it long enough, it's going to be too bitter, but I probably won't mind. That's the Asian in me."

I ask him if it's difficult, in a restaurant, to deal with the variability in sorghum syrups from season to season, boil to boil.

"Here's the thing," he answers. "Once you go down that rabbit hole of the locavore restaurant, everything becomes variable from crop to crop, year to year. Your corn is different. Your lamb is different. Your pork is different. So everything is made from scratch and everything is made 'to feel.' And when you do recipes by taste and touch, things kind of work themselves out. In some odd way, nature seems to work itself out."

Zen and the Art of
Sorghum Syrup Cookery

As I write, I have seven jars of sweet sorghum syrup on my counter from different producers in Kentucky, Tennessee, North Carolina, and Georgia. They range in color from tawny gold to a deep teak brown. One small jar of the Sugar Drip variety came crystallized, while the others have viscosities ranging from maple syrup quick to, well, slow as molasses in wintertime. Each one tastes and smells somewhat different from the other, including the two jars that are from the same farm, same crop, same year, but one was processed over steam and the other over wood fire.

Loving sorghum syrup is a lot like loving great wine: you learn to savor impermanence and variability.

Chefs like Edward Lee and Ouita Michel say that's part of the pleasure of cooking with sorghum. "I love the Zen of it," Ouita laughs. "You mean you never cook with the same sorghum twice?" I ask. "That's part of the beauty," she affirms.

The differences in tastes are subtle ones, and not so great that you can't use any pure sweet sorghum syrup for another in the recipes here. But as you get accustomed to its basic flavor, some subtle element (a grassy substrata, a more pronounced mineral or buttery note) in a new sorghum may suggest a new way to pair it, a new recipe to try.

All sorghum syrup has what my mother would have called "a whang to it." That's the slightly sour taste that cozies up perfectly with the intense sweet of sorghum when it first hits the mouth. It resolves into a buttery resonance, what chefs like to call sorghum's umami, which fills the mouth in a way that no other syrup—honey, corn, maple—can.

That umami quality allows sorghum syrup to harmonize with a vast range of foods. Sweet sorghum is the Emmylou Harris of ingredients.

The recipes that follow will show you just how that works. Meanwhile, here are some tips on using sorghum in your kitchen.

Like honey, sorghum syrup will not spoil at room temperature and so doesn't need to be refrigerated after opening. In fact, refrigeration can hasten crystallization, and it makes sorghum too thick to pour, so don't do it.

Unlike honey, sorghum that occasionally crystallizes doesn't always decrystallize when you gently heat it by placing the jar in warm water or microwave. The fact that sorghum has been heated already may be why. My experience, and that of several chefs I spoke with, is that sometimes sorghum that has crystallized will dissolve to liquid when you place the jar in a pan of warm water and slowly raise the heat some, but without boiling. Other times it doesn't. In that case, crystallized sorghum is perfect to use when you're making a brine or marinade, or to spoon into coffee, or to make the Splendid Chai on page 120. Any place where the heat, liquidity, or acidity of the substance you are adding it to will melt the crystals is fair game. And the really good news is that sorghum syrup doesn't crystallize that readily in the first place.

Sorghum will keep well over a year, sometimes more, in a tightly covered jar. If you want to "freshen" older sorghum, heat the syrup gently in a heavy skillet (don't overfill) until it just begins to boil. Add a pinch of baking soda and quickly skim off the foam that rises. Both Rona Roberts and Fred Sauceman advise eating that foam, as it is delicious. And the syrup now tastes as fresh as the day it was first boiled.

Sorghum is generally sold in Mason jars or plastic jugs. The jugs allow for ease of pouring, the least messy and most accurate way of measuring sorghum into a cup or spoon. But the glass jars let you see how much and the condition of your sorghum. And jars are easier to dip a spoon into for a dollop for your biscuit or cornbread, or to use a rubber spatula to get that last good drop out. I tend to prefer the jars and was delighted to discover that there are now several types of screw-on jar lids with built-in pouring spouts available online or in specialty cooking stores. Look for one with a wide spout to accommodate sorghum syrup's thickness. (Don't buy one with that flip-top pour slot like the ones on boxes of salt. It'll be stuck to the jar top and impossible to open in no time.)

One of the best kitchen tips I received came from Chef Jay Pierce, who said that whenever he opens a jar of sorghum to use in a recipe, he makes sure to have on hand a clean cloth dampened with warm water. He wipes the rim and lid after each pour or dip to ensure no syrup residue is left to stick and harden and make it nearly impossible to open the jar again. After closing the lid, he uses the cloth to wipe down the outside of the jar, too, top to bottom. Otherwise the jar may end up sitting in a sticky scrim.

Jay also recommends having hot water on hand to warm a cup or spoon that you plan to measure in. That does seem to make the sorghum come out a little more easily and thoroughly, but I keep an assortment of very small rubber spatulas to do the same job.

You'll notice that some of the recipes include a step in which sorghum syrup is dissolved in a warm liquid ingredient before being incorporated into the whole. This isn't always vitally necessary, but it does make it a little easier and ensures a more thorough combining of ingredients than simply plopping the sorghum in.

Keeping sorghum visible on my counter is a reminder that a

drizzle of such is often a perfect finisher, particularly to grilled or fried meat and grilled or roasted vegetables. The sorghum can stand alone or be augmented with a squirt of citrus juice, a splash of vinegar, or a dusting of red chile or freshly cracked black pepper.

Send Me In, Coach!

Once you get the hang of working with it, you'll discover that sorghum syrup can be added to or used as a substitute for another ingredient in many recipes. Here are some common ones and tips for making good exchanges.

MOLASSES: Sorghum syrup can be exchanged equally for molasses in almost any recipe, and the sorghum's tart tang and more complex flavors will add another level of enjoyment. Some sorghum syrup can be sweeter than molasses, however. That's not a given—some is not. And it would not be a noticeable factor in a recipe with a lot going on, like a molasses spice cookie or barbecue sauce with lots of ingredients. But in a circumstance where molasses shines alone, you should taste the sorghum first and determine the level of sweetness, reducing the amount by a quarter if you think it may be too sweet.

HONEY: Sorghum syrup can be exchanged equally for honey in any recipe. The sweetness levels of sorghum syrup and honey are more consistently equivalent, but sorghum will add more nuance to the resulting flavor.

SUGAR: Like honey, sorghum syrup tastes sweeter than sugar in most recipes. That's a boon because you can use less with good results, although a straight across equal exchange is fine when using spoonful amounts. When I get into cups, I use about half as much sorghum, depending on how sweet I want the result to be. When baking, because sorghum will contribute more liquid to the batter, I decrease another liquid or add a bit of dry ingredient if needed. When baking cookies or quick breads, I don't worry about it.

ALCOHOL: Some recipes recommend you soak an ingredient—raisins, say—overnight in a flavorful liquor. If you don't want to add alcohol to the mix, you can use Anna's Sorghum Simple Syrup on page 122 instead.

Additional Ingredient Notes

Bacon drippings and lard: Both pork fats make appearances in the recipes in this book. They are recommended because their flavor has a deep umami of its own that matches well with sorghum syrup's. If you don't have issues about eating meat in general, or pork in particular, or certain fats, I recommend that you use them. But I urge you to seek out leaf lard that is very fresh with no preservatives or stabilizers—a product more easily found through a butcher shop or specialty market. I store my own bacon grease in a small, covered jar that I keep refrigerated. Lard may be recommended here for its high smoke point in frying, and if you choose not to use it, pick a substitute oil that also has a high smoke point.

Mayonnaise: When a recipe calls for mayonnaise, that means mayonnaise and not commercial salad dressing. Yes, I know there are those who prefer the taste of salad dressing to mayo, but the distinguishing feature between the two is that salad dressings are noticeably sweeter. Since the recipes here depend on sorghum for both sweet and additional flavors, using a sweetened salad dressing in place of mayonnaise will disrupt the balance of flavors.

New Mexico red chile: The rest of the world is finally discovering what New Mexicans have always known: the long green chiles that grow there have a remarkable taste. Late last summer I found chile roasters in the parking lot of large grocery chains in

Long Sweeteners

On the phone, Terry Hughes tells me the best time to catch him at the Olin Hughes sorghum operation is "of a morning or around lunch time." When he says the word "time," it stretches out like a long summer day in Young Harris, Georgia, where the farm lies.

It stretches again later when, talking in person, he shakes his head ruefully and says, "Seems like people just don't have the time to eat syrup now. Even if you could get it at a drive-thru window, it's so messy. Can you imagine driving down the road trying to eat you a sorghum biscuit?"

He laughs, though, because over the seventy-year span the Hughes family has been growing sweet sorghum cane and then processing syrup, they've seen its popularity wax and wane and wax again. "Does seem as if it's growing here of late," he offers modestly, "little bit more year by year."

And then he grins, "Truth is, we basically don't have to do much of anything but wait for people to come by or call. We sell out every year."

Sorghum from the jar that Terry proffers is exceptionally nuanced and delicate, traits that have won it the affection of a number of notable chefs and restaurants. Some years earlier, Terry says, Linton Hopkins of Atlanta's revered Restaurant Eugene took a case to New York for a southern showcase he was preparing there. Pretty soon the Hughes family was shipping orders to New York City to the likes of Gramercy Tavern and Salvation Taco at Pod 39. The Early Girl and King Daddy's Chicken and Waffle in Asheville are now customers as well.

Hughes sorghum syrup's "sudden" success has been seven decades in the making. That's when Terry's dad, Olin, started a stand of cane as a young sharecropper on a place just up the road. "My mother's brother, on the Bridges side, he cooked Dad's syrup for him then." His father hauled the cane to a local mill to be pressed, as did many of his neighbors.

"It was a horse-drawn mill," Terry says. "Took a team to pull it. Back then there were thirty or forty operations, sixty thousand gallons processed in Union County annually." Young Harris is just up the road from Blairsville, where the sorghum-making tradition of this pocket in the north Georgia Appalachians is celebrated at a festival every year.

By 1949 Terry's parents had their own farm and mill and had built a screened shed where they did their own boiling. During season, they cooked three hundred to four hundred gallons daily, Olin at one evaporating table, his wife, Lois, at a second. "He'd process ten thousand gallons a year. All of it wouldn't be what he grew. He'd buy cane from his neighbors," Terry recalls.

Terry learned the art by watching and working with his parents. "There's nothing set in stone about syrup making." He notes that the color, taste, and viscosity depend on many variables, including the weather in a given year, the soil. He also notes that the work is hard.

"If you're the syrup cooker, once they light the burner, it's just like going to jail. They slam that door, you're there until the syrup's done."

But as he walks around the evaporating pan he learned on, that's still used, his hand touches it affectionately. It looks like a small, elegant piece of architecture, I say, and Terry nods and grins.

Terry says he will ship if you contact the farm by phone and he has sorghum in stock, "but I can't guarantee anything before the season, even to the restaurants. Best thing is just to come on over during season. If you're here and I've got syrup for sale and you're next in line, then you're gonna get it."

Asheville, North Carolina; Nashville, Tennessee; and Louisville, Kentucky. And roasted, canned Hatch and Mesilla green chiles are available nearly everywhere. Less known, but coming up on the horizon, is New Mexico red chile. This is the same pepper but allowed to ripen fully on the vine to a deep, succulent red, then strung in *ristras*, and dried. Dried pods can be crushed by the cook at home and used to make a blender sauce, but the easiest form for finding New Mexico red outside of New Mexico is already ground into a fine and fragrant powder.

That ground chile is what I specify in a number of recipes in the book to add not only heat but also a characteristic resonance. In many recipes I note that you can substitute cayenne, but you will be missing something subtle if you do. In the recipe for New Mexico Red Chile Sauce on page 59, no other ground chile will do.

Look for New Mexico red chile at a store that carries fine spices and seasonings or in a local market with a strong selection of Hispanic foods. If you can't find it locally, it is well worth seeking out and ordering online. I buy mild red chile, "mild" being an old New Mexico term for "plenty hot." If it's not, you can always add a little of your favorite hot sauce.

Smoked Spanish paprika: This is not your Hungarian Mama's paprika. Smoked Spanish paprika has not only its nominative wood-smoked flavor to commend it but also an umami element that tastes remarkably like bacon. This should be available from any food store that makes a point of offering high quality spices and seasonings. Or you may want to order it online. You'll be glad you did. It is an excellent addition to any meat or stew, is grand in scrambled eggs and omelets, and in the heart of summer, I mix a couple of dashes into the mayonnaise I spread on tomato sandwiches for a vegetarian BLT.

Long Sweeteners

John Fleer

When Chef John Fleer opened Rhubarb in downtown Asheville, North Carolina, in the winter of 2013, he stocked the kitchen with extra-large jugs of Muddy Pond sorghum syrup. The chef with the easy smile grins big when he says, "I wouldn't have a restaurant without it."

But such was not the case when he first arrived at Blackberry Farm, the Smoky Mountain inn where he not only made his name but also awakened the professional culinary world to such glories of the Southern Appalachian larder as Benton's hams and bacon and Cruze Farm buttermilk. The year was 1992.

"I was twenty-eight and I was determined to create a menu that reflected this unique place I was in, so I was in a process of learning and discovery," he says.

Fleer (which is what his colleagues call him) grew up in the piedmont, in Winston-Salem, North Carolina, and his mother was from the tidewater of Virginia.

"What I ate as a child was defined by her part of Virginia: lots of ham, Brunswick Stew. It was southern but not mountain, and mountain was new territory for me."

He was at a local produce market, the Horn of Plenty, in Maryville, Tennessee, when he saw a jar on the shelf that said "sorghum molasses." "The only time we used molasses when I was growing up was in ginger snaps, and we used blackstrap. This didn't look anything like blackstrap, so I bought a jar out of curiosity."

continued

When he opened it and first sniffed, then tasted, "It was a revelation. It captures such a range of flavors, gentle sweet, but so rich. So much more subtle and versatile than regular molasses, or even other syrups and sweeteners."

In the restaurant kitchen, he began subbing it where he had used honey and molasses. "My first experiments were with sweet applications, in desserts, and ham glaze. That led me to realize it's a complement to other meats. We use it in a glaze for roasted quail, duck."

And from there it was on to vegetables. Green beans dressed with sorghum syrup, red-wine vinegar, and bacon drippings show up on his menus with regularity, but lightly cooked, not long simmered in the southern tradition. "The sorghum works with that crisp bean because it's fresh itself, but it still resonates."

Fleer urges his cooks, bakers, and barkeeps to experiment with sorghum infusions—adding a spice, herb, or other flavoring element to the sorghum and heating it very gently. "I don't have a specific time for that because it just depends on the flavor and what you want to use it for. We heat it very gently, probably don't let it get above 140°F. And then we taste constantly until it reaches the state we want for what we're making. That's what I would tell cooks at home to do, too."

At Canyon Kitchen at Lonesome Valley in Cashiers, North Carolina, Fleer's other current restaurant, his encouragement led his pastry chef, Chelsea Rabe, to create an infusion using pipe tobacco for a caramel sauce for a "Gentleman's Cake." That memory provokes the grin again. "Think about it, how pipe tobacco smells. It's a perfect combination."

That first jar of sorghum Fleer found was from a producer in Kentucky, but it set him on a quest to find the syrup closer to Blackberry Farm in the foothills of the Smokies in Tennessee. "Lucky me," he says. "I discovered one of the finest sorghum producers was right in the vicinity, the Guenthers at Muddy Pond."

"It didn't occur to me that there would be different varieties of sorghum," Fleer says. "It's been another revelation of how strongly the flavor is affected by where the plant is grown, who processes it. It is a lot like wine, and we play with that."

In the bar at Rhubarb, for example, Fleer stocks a variety of sorghum syrup made in western North Carolina "because it's got a darker tone, a slight bitter edge reminiscent of blackstrap, and that works really well in cocktails.

"But Muddy Pond still is and I expect will always be my favorite," he says. "It's just elegant. Winey. Beautiful. Aromatic." And then he stops talking and just smiles.

Basics

Gravy Horse

The name for this ubiquitous mountain morning condiment comes from Balis Ritchie, folksinger Jean Ritchie's father. She writes, "Dad would take his whole meal on it, just about. He would take a big spoonful of molasses and let it run thick and slow over fresh-churned butter in a dish, then he'd take his fork and mix and stir, make Gravy Horse to eat on his cornbread. Hot cornbread, or biscuits, either one would go with fine."

Not much to add to that perfect description, but for first timers, here are some proportions and hints for making what my family just called "sorghum butter."

1 tablespoon butter
2 tablespoons sorghum syrup

Put the butter in a small bowl or saucer and let sit at room temperature until it is softened but not runny. Pour sorghum over the top and use the tines of a fork to first mash then gently whip together. You can use the fork to daub it onto hot biscuits, and this should be enough to grace a half-dozen of Ouita's Biscuits (page 63) or for dressing up Real Cornbread (page 64).

A HORSE OF A DIFFERENT FLAVOR

This recipe lends itself well to variations. For Thanksgiving, I like to make up a batch with ½ pound (2 sticks) butter, 1½ cups sorghum, and 2 tablespoons of crystallized ginger, minced. We spoon this into small-to-medium sized baked sweet potatoes still in their jackets. Makes enough to sauce 8.

You can do the same using ground New Mexico red chile instead of, or in addition to, the ginger. Start with ¼ teaspoon, adding more to taste. Use that mixture to spike the mashed flesh of a roasted winter squash.

Famed guitarist and country music legend Chet Atkins told me that he liked to get a little fancy and mix his sorghum with peanut butter. I tried it and discovered a new and more delicate rendition of the classic peanut butter and banana sandwich. The proportions are different when using peanut butter: 1 tablespoon peanut butter to 1 teaspoon of sorghum. Spread this on good whole wheat bread and then slice a ripe banana on top. I know it sounds curious, but it's delicious and surprising to sprinkle a very few fresh green alfalfa sprouts on that.

Peanut butter and sorghum marry in a surprising and delicious way in Citrus Sorghum Asian Noodles (page 100).

Orange Sorghum Vinegar

I fiddled with this recipe a little to see if I could come up with something jazzier, but every time I added something it seemed to subtract from the end result. I finally realized that this straight simple condiment was itself perfectly balanced.

You will see it referenced in several recipes in the book. I often add a splash to soup on its way to the table, or combine it with mayonnaise for a light, bright chicken or tuna salad. I've even taken a sip when I feel a cold coming on.

Make it in a small quantity to keep it tasting fresh. I put leftovers in a small covered jar in the refrigerator, but I can't tell you how long it will last since I use it up within a matter of days.

¼ cup white wine vinegar

1 tablespoon sorghum syrup

1 tablespoon fresh-squeezed orange juice

Pour vinegar into a small glass jar with lid. Add sorghum and shake or stir until dissolved. Add orange juice and shake or stir to combine. Use as directed in recipes and store any left over covered in the refrigerator.

Sorghum Caramel Sauce

This simple caramel is easy to make and a wonderful way to dress up a warm pudding or cobbler or even to add a touch of sweet to something a little more savory. Chef Ouita Michel, who shared the technique, likes to put a bit of bourbon in hers—about ½ tablespoon should do—before adding the butter. And like Ouita, I think it's divine on Woodford Pudding (page 144), the old Kentucky treat.

1 cup sorghum syrup
½ pound (2 sticks) butter, chilled, cut in pieces

In a small, heavy saucepan warm the sorghum over low heat to thin it. Remove from heat and whisk in butter, a piece at a time, until it forms a rich caramel sauce. Serve immediately or store in a tightly closed jar in the refrigerator for up to a week. Before using, bring caramel to room temperature or slightly warmer by immersing the jar in warm water.

Lucky Sorghum Glaze

Executive Chef Jay Pierce kept a shelf filled with jars of sorghum syrup in the pantry of Lucky 32 in Greensboro, North Carolina. His sorghum glaze is a versatile reduction that lends itself to adaptation. The pinch of black pepper in his version provides just a hint of hot; to up that ante, you can stir in a dash of Tabasco. A bit of cinnamon instead, and you have the perfect drizzle for baked apples; some cumin and ground red chile—well, you get the idea. But the basics start here.

1 cup sorghum syrup
⅓ cup apple cider vinegar
Pinch of freshly cracked black pepper

Simmer all ingredients in a saucepan over medium heat, stirring at first to dissolve the sorghum. When bubbles in the sauce are the size of a dime and the sauce coats the back of a spoon, remove from heat and allow to cool. Makes 1 cup.

Jay uses this to finish the Grilled Carolina Peaches with Sorghum Glaze on page 96.

New Mexico Red Chile Sauce

If you're not familiar with the New Mexico red chile, you might want to see the remarks under "Additional Ingredient Notes" (page 46) before you plunge in here.

The Zen motto of New Mexico might be: You never dredge in the same red sauce twice. Part of that is the simple fact that red chiles from different regions have subtle but distinct differences in flavor. The other is that no two cooks seem to make the sauce in quite the same way. Some add spice, some use garlic, many add a little bit of honey or sugar to amplify. After more than thirty years of stirring it up, I've come to a version that is almost austere, but for one unusual addition. That's right. Sorghum syrup beats both honey and sugar for holding up the sweet-hot front. You can barely taste a hint of it here, but you would taste quite a difference without it.

What follows is my basic recipe for the sauce to be used in the Red Chile Cheese Enchiladas with Eggs (page 116). As time goes on, you may decide you want to add garlic, Mexican oregano, cumin, or other spices—but to me, simpler is best. The sauce is also a great addition to a pot of pinto beans or your version of chili. It can be drizzled over a plethora of things from plain rice to scrambled eggs to steak or pork chops. In New Mexico, it shows up on the holiday table next to the usual boat filled with turkey gravy. If your mother-in-law from Pennsylvania made the gravy, you dab a little on your mashed potatoes, eat that, smile, and tell her how good her gravy is. Then you sigh in anticipation and ladle red chile sauce on the rest.

¼ tablespoon sorghum
1½ cup warm water, plus more if needed
1 tablespoon olive oil or lard
2 tablespoons finely chopped onion
½ cup New Mexico red chile, ground
½ to 1 teaspoon salt

Dissolve sorghum in 1½ cups of water and set aside. In a skillet or sauté pan that is large enough to hold a corn tortilla, heat oil on medium low. Sprinkle in the onions and cook, stirring, for about a minute to soften and to release fragrance.

Slowly sift in the red chile powder, stirring as you do. It will clump a little, so stir with the back of your spoon to smooth it out. Slowly pour in the water-sorghum mixture, about ½ cup at a time, stirring all the while. What you're doing is making gravy, with the chile powder acting as both flavor and thickening agent. When all the water has been added, add salt. Continue to cook and stir over medium-low heat for about 5 minutes. The mixture will begin to bubble and thicken. If it thickens too quickly, add some additional water, about 1 tablespoon at a time. When it reaches the consistency of thin— but not watery—gravy, remove it from the heat. It will continue to thicken a little bit, but you want it to be workable for immersing the tortillas to make the enchiladas on page 116.

Slow Cooker Apple Butter

Mutsu apples, Arkansas Blacks, Macouns: I can go a little crazy at apple harvest time, and finding myself with a small mountain piling up in the kitchen last autumn, I sent out a call for a great slow cooker recipe for applesauce that I could adapt to sorghum specs. Cookbook author and pal Sheri Castle grew up in the same North Carolina mountains I live in now, and so she knew a thing or two about what to do. Her splash of cider vinegar to finish is utterly inspired. This is her recipe with my sorghum syrup addition. You can start this just before you go to bed and wake up to a house that smells like heaven. It will taste like it, too, when you spoon fresh, warm, sorghum-tinged apple butter on a hot biscuit!

5½ pounds mixed apples, peeled, cored, and cut into 1-inch chunks
2 cups sugar
3 teaspoons ground cinnamon
½ teaspoon ground mace
½ teaspoon ground cardamom
¼ teaspoon ground cloves
½ teaspoon ground allspice
½ teaspoon kosher salt
1 cup sorghum syrup
2 to 3 tablespoons unfiltered organic apple cider vinegar

Place the apples in a 6-quart slow cooker. In a small bowl, stir together sugar, spices, and salt, and then pour slowly and evenly over the apples. Cover and cook on high for 1 hour, then stir in the sorghum syrup. Reduce the heat to low and cook for 8 to 10 more hours, or until the apples are completely soft and broken down. They will lose at least ⅓ of their volume. Remove the lid, stir, and increase the heat to high, and cook until almost all the liquid has evaporated, about 1 hour. Stir in the vinegar.

Purée in a food processor or blender, or directly in the cooker with an immersion blender. Serve immediately, or transfer to hot, sterilized jars and store in the refrigerator 6 to 8 weeks. Makes 3 to 4 pints.

Breads and Breakfast

Ouita's Biscuits

This recipe for perfect biscuits comes from Chef Ouita Michel, who proffers them for breakfast at Windy Corner near Paris, Kentucky. There's no sorghum syrup in them, but that's because you're supposed to slather Gravy Horse (sorghum butter, page 55) on them to your heart's content. They are also the base for her spectacular Berry Shortcakes with Sorghum Crème Fraîche on page 138.

2 cups flour
2 teaspoons baking powder
½ teaspoon baking soda
½ teaspoon salt
1 teaspoon sugar
¼ pound (1 stick) unsalted butter, chilled or frozen
¾ cup buttermilk

In a large bowl, sift together flour, baking powder, baking soda, salt, and sugar. Using a cheese grater, grate butter into dry ingredients and mix lightly with fingers until crumbly.

Add buttermilk and quickly work into flour mixture with a pastry cutter, wooden spoon, or by hand. Knead with a few quick strokes into a rounded mound and let rest 20 to 30 minutes in the refrigerator.

Heat oven to 400°F. Lightly grease or line a baking sheet with parchment paper and set aside.

Roll dough on a floured surface to a thickness of ½ inch. Cut with a 2-inch biscuit cutter and transfer to prepared baking sheet. Bake 10 to 12 minutes or until lightly browned and baked through.

Real Cornbread

No, sirree! There is not one drop of sweet sorghum syrup in this cornbread because (repeat after me, please), if God had meant for cornbread to have sugar in it, he'd have called it cake. It's been over thirty years now since I wrote those words to open an essay in *Esquire* on making real cornbread and I haven't changed my allegiance since. But while my people don't hold with sweetness in their cornbread, we are just fine with those who want to pour sweetness on, particularly when that pour is sweet sorghum syrup.

You can also slather on some Gravy Horse (page 55), but let me tell you that I didn't know people put butter on cornbread until I went to college and saw it happen in the cafeteria. That's because the bacon drippings or butter in the recipe are unctuous enough without adding on. But if that's how you roll, be my guest. This recipe is here as well because Real Cornbread is the perfect accompaniment to so many of the dishes in this book.

Cornbread is at its absolute best baked in a cast-iron skillet, and everybody should have one. If you don't, make do with a cake pan this time and then go get one. Your skillet can be 9 to 10½ inches in diameter. The smaller skillet will make a softer center, the larger more crust and will cook a little faster. Season your skillet before using it.

Yes, you can use yellow cornmeal; my people prefer white. Stone-ground is fine, the fresher the better.

4 tablespoons bacon drippings or butter
2 cups finely ground white cornmeal
1 teaspoon salt
½ teaspoon baking soda
½ teaspoon baking powder
1 egg
1½ cups milk or buttermilk, plus a little more, if needed

Heat oven to 450°F.

Put bacon drippings or butter in the skillet and put the skillet in the oven to allow the drippings to melt and the pan to heat for maximum crisping. Check the pan periodically to ensure that the drippings don't smoke or the butter blacken. Don't take the skillet out until it makes an inviting crackling noise when you very, very carefully swirl the fat. (Do not try to heat the skillet and grease on a burner on the stove top, as that will create irregular hot spots in the bottom of the pan, to which the cornbread will stick.)

In a large bowl, combine cornmeal, salt, baking soda, and baking powder. Break an egg in the center of the meal and break the yolk and stir it just a little bit. Add the milk and stir to incorporate.

When the skillet and drippings are ready, take the pan from the oven and swirl the fat gently to coat a little up the sides of the skillet, then pour the drippings into the cornbread batter, leaving just a bit in the pan; set the hot pan aside. Stir the batter and, if necessary, add more milk to achieve proper consistency. The batter should be pourably liquid but not thin.

Pour the batter into the hot skillet, put it into hot oven, and wait 20 to 25 minutes, until center is firm and edges are just browning. If the crust is not sufficiently browned on top, run it under the broiler for a few seconds.

Serve from the skillet or turn pan upside down over a big plate and cornbread should come right out. Serve while it's hot. Serves 6.

Oh! Oh! Oatmeal Bread

The seduction begins with this loaf in the oven, filling your kitchen with buttery sweet fragrance. It continues with the sight of that golden brown crust. It's difficult, but you really must wait before slicing because this bread is very tender and light, despite 2 cups of whole wheat flour. It's great for sandwiches and perfect for toast. And no one would look askance if you wanted to eat every bite with only Gravy Horse (page 55) on top!

2 packages active dry yeast

1 teaspoon sugar

2 cups water, divided

1 cup rolled oats

5⅓ tablespoons butter

⅓ cup sorghum syrup, plus a little more

1 tablespoon salt

1 egg

2 cups whole wheat flour

2½ to 3 cups unbleached flour or bread flour, divided

Dissolve yeast and sugar in 1 cup of lukewarm water. Let stand for 10 minutes, then stir well—it should be foamy on top. (If it's not, buy new yeast.) Set aside. Bring the remaining 1 cup of water to a boil and pour it into a large bowl. Add oats, butter, sorghum, and salt. Let the mixture stand 5 minutes to cool and then stir to blend evenly. Add egg and beat well.

Add whole wheat flour to oats mixture and stir to incorporate. Add the yeast and water mixture and stir in. Add 2 cups of the unbleached flour, and stir with a wooden spoon until a soft dough forms. Sprinkle ½ cup flour on a clean counter and turn the dough out of the bowl onto surface. Knead with floured hands, adding enough of the remaining flour to keep the dough from being too sticky to handle.

Knead until the dough is smooth, soft, and a tiny bit sticky, about 10 minutes. Form dough into a ball and transfer to an oiled large bowl, turning to coat. Cover bowl with plastic wrap and allow the dough to rise at warm room temperature until doubled in bulk, 1½ to 2 hours. (You can also refrigerate it overnight, but take it out and allow it to come to room temperature before working with it again.)

Lightly butter two 8½-by-4½-inch loaf pans. Turn out dough onto a lightly floured surface and knead several times to remove air. Divide dough in half and shape each half into a loaf, then place each in a pan. Drape a kitchen towel over the pans and set aside until the loaves have risen nearly to the top of the pans, about 1 hour.

Heat oven to 350°F, and place oven rack in the middle position in the oven. Mix about 1 teaspoon of sorghum with a little water and brush the tops of the loaves with the mixture (it will help the loaves brown). Bake 50 to 60 minutes. Bread should be lightly browned and sound hollow when tapped on the bottom.

Transfer to a rack to cool completely, about 1½ hours. Slice with a serrated knife.

Spice and Sorghum Loaf

The Jewish New Year celebration, Rosh Hashanah, typically includes a spice and honey cake to symbolize the sweetness possible in the coming year. Sorghum simply adds an extra resonance to that flavor. This not-too-moist loaf is delicious with tea or coffee to greet the morning or a glass of wine or good whiskey to toast new beginnings.

⅔ cup sugar

2 eggs

2 tablespoons coconut (or vegetable) oil

⅔ cup sorghum syrup

2¼ cups flour

1 teaspoon baking powder

1 teaspoon baking soda

½ teaspoon salt

1 teaspoon ground coriander

1 teaspoon allspice

½ cup warm water

Walnut pieces or pecans (optional)

Preheat oven to 350°F. Grease and flour a loaf pan and set aside. Cream sugar and eggs, then blend in oil and sorghum.

Sift flour with other dry ingredients, including spices. Add about ⅓ to sorghum mixture and blend. Add half the water and blend. Repeat until all flour and water are incorporated.

Pour into loaf pan and sprinkle nuts on top, if desired. Bake for 45 minutes and check to see if top is browning too quickly. If so, cover with tented aluminum foil. Lower temperature to 325°F and bake an additional 15 minutes until cake tests done.

Allow to cool on rack. Use the side of a knife to loosen from the loaf pan, and invert on rack. Serve immediately or wrap well in plastic wrap to keep.

Sweetly Chewy, Seedy, Fruity, Aromatic Loaf

This easy-to-make luscious bread manages to be both earthy and light at the same time. Its seductive flavor pairs with tea or coffee but is also a fine foil for a luncheon sandwich with chicken or an assortment of cheeses.

2 cups rye flour

1 cup cornmeal (white or yellow)

2 teaspoons baking soda

1 teaspoon salt

1 tablespoon fennel

1 cup dried Turkish apricots, chopped raisin size

¼ cup fresh-squeezed tangerine juice (about 2 tangerines)

¾ cup milk

1 teaspoon apple cider vinegar

1 cup sorghum syrup

Heat oven to 350°F. Grease the inside of a 9-by-5-inch loaf pan and set aside.

In a large bowl, combine the flour, cornmeal, soda, and salt. Add the fennel and apricots and stir to distribute well.

In a separate bowl, mix together tangerine juice, milk, and

vinegar—it may curdle slightly. Add sorghum and stir until completely blended. Pour the liquid into the flour mixture and stir until just blended well. Pour into loaf pan and bake for 1 hour.

Test with toothpick or knife inserted in center; if it comes out clean, the bread is done. Allow to cool in pan on rack for a few minutes, then run a table knife around inner edge of pan to separate. Invert pan over rack and shake gently until bread slides out. Turn over and allow to cool completely on rack before slicing. Serve plain or toasted.

Cheesy Spicy Muffins

Sweet sorghum is the perfect facilitator to bring cheese and spice together in this lovely, sconelike muffin.

2 cups flour
3 teaspoons baking powder
¼ teaspoon baking soda
½ teaspoon salt
¼ teaspoon cinnamon
¼ teaspoon allspice
¼ teaspoon ground coriander
½ cup milk
½ cup sorghum syrup
¼ cup coconut oil
¾ cup grated aged gouda cheese

Heat oven to 375°F. Lightly spray 12 muffin cups with oil and set aside.

Sift the first seven ingredients together in a large bowl and set aside. Warm the milk in a small pan on low heat; stir in sorghum to dissolve. Add coconut oil (if it has solidified, you can continue to warm to liquefy). Pour contents of the pan into flour mixture, stirring to incorporate. When blended, fold in cheese. Fill muffin cups ¾ full and bake for 15 to 20 minutes. Makes 1 dozen.

Kentucky Cakes 2.0

I came up with the prototype, what I now call Kentucky Cakes 1.0, in my first cookbook and have spent many a breakfast over the last twenty-five years refining. It's time for the second generation, with sorghum, to debut.

The best way to get the cup of cornbread that this recipe requires is to make a skillet of Real Cornbread (page 64) for supper the night before and set aside a cup of crumbled bread. If you make a skillet full just for the sake of these cakes, you can freeze the remaining cornbread in one-cup increments, crumbled, and you will be set the next time you want these for breakfast. Or you can stockpile frozen cornbread to make cornbread dressing.

---

4 pieces of bacon
Fried Apples (page 95)
1 cup crumbled cornbread
1 cup flour
1 teaspoon salt
1 teaspoon baking powder
2 eggs
2 tablespoons sorghum syrup
2 cups buttermilk, divided
Vegetable oil for frying
½ to 1 teaspoon bourbon (optional)

In a heavy skillet, preferably cast iron, fry the bacon until nice and crisp. Remove bacon from skillet to drain and remove skillet from heat; pour drippings into cup and set aside.

Prepare fried apples and keep slightly warm.

In a large bowl, place cornbread, and ensure crust is broken into small pieces. Sift together flour, salt, and baking powder and incorporate with cornbread.

Break eggs into a small bowl and whisk once or twice to begin blending yolk and white, then whisk in sorghum, 1 tablespoon of the bacon drippings, and 1 cup of the buttermilk. Add this to the dry ingredients and stir, adding additional buttermilk as needed to make a wet, just pourable batter. Crumble or cut bacon pieces and mix into the batter.

In the same skillet you used for frying bacon, pour enough vegetable oil or remaining drippings to lightly coat the pan, and place on medium heat. Oil should become hot but not smoking. Ladle batter into pan to make cakes 3 to 5 inches across. When bubbles start to form on the top of the batter and the edges get firm and look a little glazed, flip the cake. Cook until done. (Test by lightly pressing your finger in the middle of the cake. If it feels spongy and springy as opposed to squishy, liquidy, it's ready.)

Serve topped with fried apples. If you like, add a splash of bourbon to the apples just before topping the cakes with them. Serves 4 nicely and 2 piggishly.

Sorghum and Sorghum Gluten-Free Sweet Potato Waffles

My daughter, Meghan, has become the mother of invention when it comes to breakfast for my grandson. Finn has wheat intolerance, but that's no problem with creations like this coming from the kitchen! Several good gluten-free flour blends are available at most groceries these days, as is sorghum flour. You may also use wheat flour if it's not an issue and you'd prefer.

1 cup gluten-free flour mix

1 cup sorghum flour

2 teaspoons baking powder

2 teaspoons cinnamon

½ teaspoon ground ginger

½ teaspoon ground cloves

1 cup cooked sweet potato, mashed

1½ cups milk

2 tablespoons sorghum syrup

2 tablespoons coconut oil, liquefied

1 egg

In a large bowl, sift together flours, baking powder, and spices. In another bowl, blend together sweet potato, milk, sorghum, oil, and egg. Pour the wet ingredients into the dry and mix. It will form a thick batter. Let the mixture rest for about 10 minutes. Then heat waffle iron and pour batter in according to your iron's specification. These may take a little longer to crisp than usual, but are so worth the wait. Serve hot topped with ginger sorghum butter (see A Horse of a Different Flavor, page 55). Serves 4.

Egg McMountain

The tangy bite of arugula and the salty energy of country ham underscored by the sweet comfort of sorghum syrup—what a way to wake up!

For each serving:

Handful of arugula
1 teaspoon apple cider vinegar
Salt and black pepper
1 English muffin
1 thin slice country ham or *jamón serrano*
Oil to lightly coat pan
1 egg
1 tablespoon sorghum syrup, to drizzle

Toss arugula with vinegar and salt and pepper to your liking. Set aside.

Split the English muffin using a fork. (This makes lots of little ridges for the sorghum drizzle, while a knife just makes plateaus.) Toast.

While muffin is toasting, quickly warm ham in a skillet on medium, taking care not to brown. When ham is just warmed, remove from skillet and add enough oil to skillet to lightly coat the surface. Fry egg in the oil until white is set but yolk is still runny.

When muffin is done, lay halves next to one another on plate with cut sides up, and drizzle sorghum on each. Lay ham over muffin halves and spread arugula over ham. Place the fried egg on top. Eat immediately.

Toast Caribe

Back in the day, a long-haired, widely traveled friend taught me to spread ripe mashed banana on toast and top with a sprinkle of black pepper. He swore this was what folks had for breakfast in Jamaica. Or the Bahamas. Or some mysterious cay. He was never all that accurate with where he'd been; but he was right that the toast was tasty. Add in butter and a drizzle of sorghum syrup and it becomes downright divine.

2 slices whole-grain bread
Butter
1 very ripe banana, peeled and mashed
Sorghum syrup
Black pepper

Toast bread and slather with butter. Spread each piece with ½ of the banana. Drizzle sorghum syrup in fine line to just flavor. Add a few grinds of fresh black pepper.

Soups, Salads, and Dressings

Curried Pumpkin Soup

This can be served as is, but it is also delightful topped with a dollop of plain yogurt and Pear and Dried Cranberry Chutney (page 97).

2 tablespoons butter
1 cup chopped onion
1 tablespoon minced peeled fresh ginger
1 tablespoon curry powder
1 quart vegetable or chicken broth
1 tablespoon sorghum syrup
2 (15-ounce) cans pumpkin purée
1½ cups light coconut milk
Salt and cayenne

In a soup pot on medium heat, melt butter. Add onions and cook until they soften and begin to turn translucent. Add ginger and curry powder and heat, stirring, to release fragrance, about 1 minute or less. Add the broth, and as it begins to warm, stir in the sorghum until it dissolves. Add the pumpkin purée and coconut milk, mixing well to blend. Turn heat to low and simmer uncovered for 30 minutes, stirring from time to time to prevent sticking. Add salt and cayenne to taste. Serves 6.

Fragrant Winter Squash Soup

This is a delicate soup with a subtle, delightful flavor that changes depending on the squash. Acorn and butternut are fine choices, but lately so many interesting winter squash are available that I recommend you experiment. I like the soft, buttery pieces of sautéed onion suspended in the velvety emulsion, but if you don't, you can process them with the rest of the ingredients.

2½ to 3 pounds winter squash
⅓ cup dried lemongrass
1 tablespoon sorghum syrup
1 cup boiling water
1 cup light unsweetened coconut milk
3 tablespoons butter
1 medium sweet onion, peeled and chopped (about 1 cup)
½ teaspoon coriander
¾ teaspoon salt
Fresh fennel fronds for garnish

Preheat oven to 450°F. Pierce the skin of the squash 3 or 4 times and place on middle rack in oven. Put a pan or foil on the lower rack to catch drips. Roast for 1 to 1½ hours until flesh is soft to pressure from fingers. The time will vary depending on the type of squash and thickness of flesh and rind.

When squash is tender, remove from oven and allow to cool while you make the lemongrass infusion. To do this, place lemongrass in a teapot or heatproof glass pitcher or jar. Pour water over the dried lemongrass. Allow to steep for 15 minutes, then strain, discarding the lemongrass. Dissolve the sorghum in the warm liquid and pour into blender.

Split squash lengthwise and remove seeds and strings. Peel, or scoop out the flesh. Add approximately 3 cups lightly mashed squash to the infusion in the blender. A little more or less will not hurt. Add coconut milk and process until all is blended together.

Melt butter on medium-high in a heavy 2-quart pot. Add onions and sauté at a lively pace until just turning golden and the butter is barely beginning to brown. Remove from heat and add coriander, tossing to warm. Add the squash purée and salt, stir, and return pot to heat, turning low. Stir and heat until just steaming, then remove from heat and cover the pot. Let the flavors mingle for about 10 minutes before serving.

Fill bowls and garnish with snipped fronds of fresh fennel. Serves 6.

Bittersweet Root and Rainbow Chard Stew

This is a bracing, sustaining vegan stew that serves excellently as a main course with bread, but it can also work as a side. It fits into the transition times between seasons when root veggies and chard are still abundant. I use turnip and carrot, but you may play with other choices including beets and creamy gold potatoes as substitutes for all or half. The chard works better than other, brassier greens, however, in part for its more delicate flavor and also for the extra color of its rainbow stems.

This stew is made in several distinct steps as opposed to dumping everything in the pot at once. Making additions at just the right point in the process creates a subtly layered flavor.

1 large bunch fresh rainbow chard
Oil
1 cup chopped white onion
1 garlic clove, minced
1 tablespoon minced peeled fresh ginger
2 teaspoons ground coriander
½ teaspoon smoked Spanish paprika
2 cups water
1 sweet potato, peeled and diced
1 teaspoon salt
3 cups mixed turnips and carrots, thumbnail-sized dice
1 teaspoon sorghum syrup

½ cup warm water
1 tablespoon tamari
1 teaspoon apple cider vinegar
Salt and pepper

Rinse the chard and remove stems from leaves. Trim stems and chop into thumbnail-sized dice. Cut leaves into strips about ½-inch wide and 3 inches long. Set aside.

Pour enough oil to coat the bottom of a large pot. Place over medium heat and sauté onion until it just begins to soften. Add garlic and ginger, stir, and let cook about 1 minute. Add coriander and paprika and heat, stirring, for 1 minute more.

Add water, diced sweet potato, and salt and bring to a boil. Cover, turn heat down to a lively simmer, and cook for about 15 minutes, until potatoes are very soft. Use a potato masher or heavy wooden spoon to mash the potatoes lightly to make a chunky slurry.

Add the mixed turnips and carrots, allow the mixture to resume a lively simmer, cover, and cook for 10 minutes. Add the chard stems, stirring to mix in, cover, and cook for another 5 minutes, or until stems and roots are tender but not overly cooked. You still want a little al dente resilience.

Dissolve sorghum in warm water, add tamari and apple cider vinegar, and stir into the pot. Add chard leaves and stir until they are all submerged. Cover and simmer for 10 more minutes.

Remove pot from heat, stir well, cover, and allow to sit for about 10 minutes before serving. You may add salt and black pepper to taste at this point, or do that individually at the table.

Serves 4 as a hearty main course with bread or 6 to 8 as a starter or side.

Arugula Fennel Citrus Salad

The sharp bite of the arugula and heady licorice of the fennel are perfectly underscored by the sweet sorghum citrus of the vinegar. I have made and served this with a vinaigrette including oil but also simply with additional Orange Sorghum Vinegar and no oil. It's delicious either way.

4 cups arugula

1 bulb fresh fennel

Supremes from 1 orange

1 tablespoon Orange Sorghum Vinegar (page 56), or more to
taste

2 tablespoons olive oil (optional)

Salt and black pepper

Rinse and dry arugula and place in a large salad bowl. Trim the
fennel of end and stems, reserving fronds and bulb. Remove outer
layer from bulb if blemished. Halve and then slice thin crescents. Add
to arugula along with the orange supremes and toss a couple of times
to distribute. Mince enough fennel fronds for 1 tablespoon. Mix with
vinegar and oil and toss with arugula to coat. Salt and pepper to taste
and serve immediately. Serves 4.

Soul of Summer Fruit Salad

It goes without saying that this salad is at its best when all the fruit is at
the peak of ripeness. Curiously, the vinegar brings out the sweetness of
the fruit while the sorghum gives it an undercurrent of drama.

Sometimes the farmers market has smaller melons, a little bigger
than a softball. It's fun then to combine the peaches and cherries, and a
little less vinegar, and serve it individually in melon halves.

2 cups peeled and sliced fresh peaches

2 cups cherries, halved and pitted

2 cups peeled and diced honeydew or other ripe melon

2 tablespoons Orange Sorghum Vinegar (page 56)

¼ cup fresh mint, minced, plus 4 to 6 sprigs for garnish

In a large bowl, lightly toss together the fruit, vinegar, and mint.
Serve in individual bowls with mint sprig garnish. Serves 4 to 6.

Aromatic Broccoli and Hearts of Palm Salad

Broccoli salad is such a great concept, but raw broccoli is a chewy reality. Barely blanching the florets keeps crispness, heightens the color, and helps the aromatic sorghum dressing cozy up with the broccoli. The onion and hearts of palm contribute tang and sour, so neither vinegar nor lemon are required, while the velvety sorghum means no oil need be applied. This needs to sit at least 1 hour before serving, but it's even better if you can let it be for 8 or more.

¼ cup sorghum syrup
½ teaspoon minced fresh ginger
¼ teaspoon fennel seeds
1 quart water
½ teaspoon salt
3 cups broccoli florets, thumb-sized
¼ cup diced sweet onion
½ cup hearts of palm, cut in ¼-inch deep rounds

In a large bowl, mix sorghum, ginger, and fennel to blend. Set aside.

In a pot with lid, on high heat, bring water and salt to a boil and add the broccoli florets. Cover and boil for 1½ minutes, then remove from heat and drain immediately. Mix hot broccoli with sorghum, working quickly, but making sure the broccoli gets coated. Add onion and hearts of palm, mixing quickly again. (The tiny amount of residual water on the broccoli, and its heat, will dissolve the sorghum and make the dressing watery. This is what you want.) Place bowl uncovered in refrigerator for 5 minutes to allow any steam to evaporate, then cover and let sit for at least 1 hour before serving. You can let it sit overnight as well. Serves 4.

Butter Bean and Shoepeg Salad

Alabama chef Wylie Poundstone created the prototype for this salad and shared it with me 15 years ago. It's still a favorite and is best if you can get fresh butter beans, aka baby lima beans. But Wylie noted that it needed drained, canned shoepeg corn—not fresh or frozen—for the additional sweetness that contrasts so effectively with the original cider or red wine vinegar in the dressing. Substituting Orange Sorghum Vinegar brings that sweet right to the table, however, and raises the stakes with a little bit of citrus to boot. Fresh or frozen shoepeg corn (or a small-kernel corn variety) can be used now and is both crisper and tastier than the canned.

1 cup water, divided
1¼ cups fresh or frozen baby lima beans
1¼ cups fresh or frozen white small-kernel corn
½ cup finely chopped red onion
½ cup finely chopped red bell pepper
1 teaspoon minced garlic
¼ teaspoon kosher salt
Black pepper
2 tablespoons Orange Sorghum Vinegar (page 56)
¼ cup mayonnaise

In a saucepan with lid, bring ½ cup of the water to a boil and add beans. Stir very gently with a spoon until the water begins to boil again, then turn heat to low, cover, and simmer until beans are al dente (the insides are tender, but the skins are intact and should pop a little when you bite into one). Fresh beans will take from 12 to 20 minutes to reach this state, depending on how fresh and how small they are. Frozen beans should take 20 to 25 minutes. Drain and place in large bowl.

Add remaining ½ cup of the water to saucepan, bring to a boil, and add the corn. When water begins to boil again, cook the corn for 3 minutes, if fresh, 6 minutes, if frozen. (The finished corn should be crisper than if you were going to sauce it for a side dish.) Drain and add corn to beans. Add onion, bell pepper, and garlic. Add salt, add pepper to taste, and toss to season.

In a small bowl, whisk vinegar into mayonnaise. When incorporated, pour onto vegetables and toss until everything is coated.

If salad is still warm, let it sit until room temperature, then cover and refrigerate for at least 2 hours before serving. Serves 8.

Rhubarb's Red Wine Sorghum Vinaigrette

This pungent vinaigrette works well in salads with equally strong ingredients. At John Fleer's Rhubarb in Asheville, they use it to meld radicchio, country ham, and goat cheese, as described below. It's also great with bitter greens enhanced by bacon and/or black walnuts. If you don't have Banyuls vinegar, substitute a good sherry vinegar or use more of the red wine vinegar.

1 tablespoon chopped shallots
¼ teaspoon chopped garlic
½ teaspoon crushed green peppercorns
½ teaspoon kosher salt
¼ cup red wine vinegar
⅛ cup Banyuls wine vinegar
1 teaspoon Dijon mustard
1 cup hazelnut oil
⅛ cup sorghum syrup

Combine shallots, garlic, peppercorns, and salt with the vinegars and let sit for 10 minutes. Whisk in mustard, then oil, then sorghum. Makes about 1½ cups and can be refrigerated, but will need to be whisked again before using.

At Rhubarb, for each salad, they dress ½ cup radicchio chiffonade and 1 tablespoon julienned fresh strawberries with vinaigrette and a dash of salt. This marinates while the chef sears a slice of fresh goat cheese, about 1½ ounces, in olive oil to caramelize each surface. The salad is served with goat cheese in the center and a thin slice of warmed country ham accompanied by cornbread croutons. A blackberry balsamic reduction and a bit of sorghum syrup are drizzled on top of the cheese.

Buttermilk Sorghum Dressing

This recipe makes enough dressing for dipping with the Sriracha Sorghum Wings on page 124. If you increase that recipe, do the same proportionately here. This is also delicious on any crisp green salad.

¾ cup buttermilk
½ tablespoon sorghum syrup
¾ cup mayonnaise
½ teaspoon salt
1 teaspoon minced celery leaves or fennel fronds
3 drops Tabasco
3 tablespoons finely minced green onion

In a bowl, whisk together buttermilk and sorghum until syrup is dissolved. Whisk in mayonnaise and salt. Add the other ingredients and whisk to blend. Cover and refrigerate until you are ready to serve.

Fruits and Vegetables

Maque Choux

Pronounced "mock shoe," this is a popular side or main dish in the Cajun country of southwestern Louisiana. When maque choux is made in the summer, fresh corn is sliced off the cob without cutting too deeply, then the remaining kernels are "milked" by running a spoon down the cob and letting the juices drip in the bowl. The resulting taste and texture is creamy. This version replicates that in the winter with frozen corn by processing part of the corn in a blender with milk. The sorghum enhances the sweetness of the corn.

This dish makes a distinctive spicy vegetable for Thanksgiving, a good foil for the sweeter players that usually fill the table. If you'd like to make it the centerpiece of a meal, you can add about 2 dozen medium-sized raw shrimp, peeled and deveined, just after you add the half-and-half. Simmer until the shrimp are just cooked.

1 (14.5-ounce) can fire-roasted whole tomatoes
½ tablespoon sorghum syrup
2 tablespoons olive oil
1 cup chopped onion
1 medium bell pepper, chopped
1 clove of garlic, crushed
16 ounces frozen corn (shoepeg or small white corn is best)
½ cup milk
1 teaspoon salt
Freshly ground black pepper

¼ teaspoon cayenne, or to taste

3 tablespoons half-and-half

Hot sauce

Drain tomatoes, reserving juice. Add sorghum to the tomato juice and stir until dissolved. Chop or tear tomatoes coarsely and set aside.

In a heavy skillet with lid, warm the olive oil over medium heat, then add the onion and bell pepper, and sauté until the onion turns translucent and the bell pepper is soft. Stir in garlic and cook for a minute or so longer.

While the vegetables cook, put 1 cup of the corn and the milk in blender and process at medium for about a minute, until the corn and milk make a thick mush but some kernels are still evident. Add the blended corn and the rest of the corn to the skillet and stir. Then add the tomatoes, the sorghum mixture, salt, and black pepper. Add the cayenne and taste, and add more as necessary. Let the mixture come to a bubbling simmer, then turn the heat low, cover, and cook for 45 minutes, stirring frequently. The mixture should be very juicy but not soupy. Add water a little at a time if there's a danger of it sticking.

After 45 minutes, add half-and-half and let simmer, uncovered, until mixture is steaming. Serve with hot sauce passed on the side. Serves 8 as side dish.

Bengali Vegetables

Many savory foods of the Bengal region are distinguished by a hint of sweetness. Sorghum syrup is the perfect medium for providing that as its tangy, dusky additional flavors work beautifully with the spices of India.

2 teaspoons sorghum syrup

½ teaspoon salt

½ cup hot water

2 tablespoons ghee or coconut oil

3 tablespoons minced fresh ginger

1 teaspoon ground cumin
½ teaspoon ground fennel
½ teaspoon celery seed
½ teaspoon ground black mustard seed
2 cups diced, unpeeled Yukon Gold potato
3 cups cauliflower florets, cut thumb size
3 cups diced yellow squash
1 (14.5-ounce) can diced fire-roasted tomatoes

Dissolve sorghum and salt in hot water and set aside.

In a heavy saucepan with lid, heat ghee, add ginger, and fry just enough to release fragrance. Add other spices and stir briskly in oil for about 1 minute.

Add the sorghum water and potatoes, stirring to cover with spice. Cover tightly and lower heat to simmer for 10 minutes. (Do not allow potatoes or other vegetables to stick; add little bits of water, if necessary, to prevent sticking, but not too much.) Stir in cauliflower, cover, and simmer for 10 minutes. Stir in squash, cover, and simmer for 5 minutes. Stir in tomatoes, cover, and simmer for 5 minutes. Remove from heat and allow to sit, covered, for 5 additional minutes. Serve immediately. Serves 4.

Spicy Sweet Potatoes

Sweet potatoes, abundant in the fall and winter, have become an essential part of holiday dinners, but the tendency to candy them beyond all semblance of a vegetable and into the realm of dessert is an insult to their essential goodness. Sorghum adds the perfect undertone to their sweetness, and when spiked with spice, this dish is ideal with turkey, goose, duck, or pork.

2 pounds of sweet potatoes
4 tablespoons butter
¼ cup sorghum syrup
1 teaspoon ground cinnamon

1 teaspoon ground allspice
⅛ teaspoon New Mexico red chile or cayenne
¼ cup crystallized ginger, chopped small

Heat oven to 400°F. Wash and dry potatoes and pierce several times with the tines of fork. Place on cookie sheet and bake until very tender, usually about 40 minutes, but fatter potatoes may take longer. Allow to cool until you can handle them, and peel. Place in a bowl and use a potato masher or large fork to mash lightly.

In a small saucepan on low heat, melt the butter and stir in sorghum to dissolve. Mix in cinnamon, allspice, and red chile, and pour over the potatoes. Mash again, incorporating the new ingredients and making the potatoes creamy. Stir in the ginger and serve immediately. Serves 4 generously.

Note: The dish can be made ahead, refrigerated covered, and warmed in microwave before serving to accommodate a holiday feast.

Squash and Apple Bake

The pepper adds a great counterpoint to the sorghum.

1 medium butternut squash, peeled, seeded, and cut in 1-inch cubes
3 medium tart green apples, cored and cut in 1-inch cubes
Salt and freshly ground black pepper
¼ cup sorghum syrup
⅓ cup dried cherries, raisins, or cranberries
2 to 3 tablespoons butter
1 tablespoon fresh lemon juice

Heat oven to 350°F. Lightly grease a 9-by-13-inch baking pan. Combine squash and apples in the pan and stir to mix. Season generously with salt and pepper.

Combine sorghum, cherries, butter, and lemon juice in a heavy small saucepan or microwave-safe dish and heat, stirring occasionally, to melt butter and combine evenly. Pour syrup over squash mix.

Cover pan with foil and bake 30 minutes. Remove foil, stir the ingredients, and cook 30 minutes more, stirring a few times and making sure to get into the corners of the pan. Turn heat down if mixture appears to be burning. Bake until squash is very tender.

Serves 6 or more.

Barbecue Boiled Peanuts

Mmmmm! Like baked beans raised to the fourth power, that's what Craig Deihl's Barbecue Boiled Peanuts taste like. The Pennsylvania native likes to mix the traditions of his home state with those of his current home, Charleston, South Carolina, where he is executive chef of Cypress. We get to eat the remarkable results.

While green peanuts are traditionally boiled in the shell, the raw peanuts in Craig's recipe are already shelled.

1 pound raw peanuts, preferably Valencias

3 quarts water

½ pound smoked bacon, cubed

1 cup diced onion

¼ cup crushed garlic

¼ cup Dijon mustard

½ cup sorghum syrup

¼ cup chili sauce

1 teaspoon ground cloves

¼ teaspoon ground allspice

1 teaspoon black pepper

In a stock pot, bring the peanuts and water to a boil. Reduce the temperature to a low simmer, cover, and cook for 2 to 3 hours or until the peanuts are tender. Remove from heat.

Heat oven to 350°F. Oil a 9-by-13-inch casserole pan.

In a skillet, over medium heat, cook the bacon to release some fat, then add the onion and cook, stirring occasionally, until translucent and soft. Add garlic and continue cooking until onions are caramelized, about 15 minutes total. Add this to the boiled peanuts and their cooking liquid, along with the remaining ingredients. Mix well. Transfer into casserole pan and cover with aluminum foil. Bake for 1 hour. Remove the foil and bake for an additional 25 minutes. Remove from oven and keep warm until you are ready to serve. Serves 8 generously.

Christmas Greens

Actually, you can eat this hearty dish any time of the year, but its festive red and green colors invoke a holiday spirit, and it makes a nice entrée on the table for vegetarians. Kale is my favorite base green and I like to throw in mustard greens or turnip greens for spice. You can use collards, chard, or spinach—choose whatever is freshest.

2 big bunches mixed greens (about 16 ounces)
2 tablespoons olive oil
1 teaspoon toasted sesame oil
½ cup chopped onion
1 teaspoon minced garlic
1 tablespoon sesame seeds
2 (14.5-ounce) cans diced tomatoes
2 cups cooked garbanzo beans, or 1 (15.5-ounce) can, drained
1 tablespoon tamari sauce
½ tablespoon sorghum syrup
¼ teaspoon balsamic vinegar
¼ teaspoon smoked Spanish paprika
1 tablespoon tahini paste
Salt and black pepper

Rinse greens well. Remove any very large stems, then tear or cut into matchbook-sized pieces. Set aside.

In a wide, deep pan with a lid, on medium heat, warm olive and sesame oils, blended. Add onions and cook until they are translucent. Add garlic and sesame seeds and cook, stirring, until seeds just start to turn a light golden color. Add the greens, a couple of handfuls at a time, stirring down into the oil and adding more as they shrink from the heat. Add tomatoes and garbanzo beans and cook, covered, about 10 minutes.

While greens mixture is cooking, in a small bowl, whisk together tamari and sorghum syrup until dissolved, then whisk in vinegar and paprika. When greens are ready, add the tamari mixture and stir, then stir in the tahini. (The tahini will stay clumped in spoon at first but as it comes in contact with the warm liquid in the pan, it will thin and disperse.) Add salt and pepper to taste. Raise heat until mixture gets bubbly, then remove from heat. Serve immediately with Real Cornbread (page 64) and your favorite hot sauce on the side. Serves 4.

Braised Greens with Pot Likker

Fresh or lightly sautéed kale and its kin have become a trend, and a delicious one, but there's an alchemical magic that creates something truly special when you braise greens—particularly piquant varieties like turnip and mustard—low and slow, southern style. The broth in the pot becomes prized pot likker, to be sopped with Real Cornbread (page 64).

6 cups water
¼ pound salt pork
2 pounds mixed greens, including generous portions of mustard and/or turnip greens
1 tablespoon sorghum syrup
2 teaspoons salt
¼ cup apple cider vinegar
Freshly cracked black pepper
1 white onion, sliced, for serving

In a large pot with lid, bring water to a boil and drop in the piece of salt pork. Turn heat to medium low, cover, and let simmer for 30 minutes to make a bacon-seasoned broth.

While simmering broth, clean greens by rinsing several times in cold water and rubbing your fingers over the surface to be sure no grit remains in the ridges. Remove stems and set aside. Tear greens into matchbook-sized pieces. Trim stems and chop into ½-inch lengths.

In a small bowl, dissolve sorghum and salt in vinegar and set aside.

When broth is ready, add greens, pushing down with a wooden spoon until all are submerged. Stir in vinegar mixture. Cover and simmer on low heat for an hour. Taste and add cracked black pepper to taste just before serving.

Greens may be served immediately or cooled and refrigerated then reheated up to 1 day later. Serve with sliced white onion and cornbread on the side.

Black Walnut Green Beans

The prized black walnut is another umami delivery system, darker in flavor with an almost bourbony undercurrent. These hard-to-extract kernels show up in rich sorghum cakes and fruit salads in the winter. Kentucky folk singer Jean Ritchie recollected that her family liked to eat them out of hand, "trading off with a bite of cornbread between bites of the black walnuts," all with a cold glass of milk. Black walnuts can also provide a mysterious, earthy tone to a bright garden vegetable such as green beans. A few contemporary chefs mix them with haricot verts or smaller green beans that are lightly steamed. They're good like that, but I like them even better with a slightly more mature bean cooked to just tender stage.

4 cups strung and broken green beans, about 1 pound
1 tablespoon bacon drippings or oil
¼ cup diced sweet onion
¼ cup black walnut pieces
1 tablespoon Orange Sorghum Vinegar (page 56) or ½ tablespoon
    apple cider vinegar mixed with ½ tablespoon sorghum syrup
Salt and black pepper

Place beans in a heavy pot with a lid, cover with water, and bring to a boil. Turn heat to medium-low and simmer for 20 to 30 minutes until beans are just tender. Drain and set aside.

In a large skillet, melt drippings or heat oil to sauté level. Add onion, and when it begins to turn transparent, add the walnut pieces and toss until just heated. Add green beans and toss to coat with oil. Remove from heat and immediately add vinegar or vinegar-sorghum mixture, stir, and add salt and pepper to taste. Serve immediately. Serves 4.

Sweet Tart Summer Squash

My mother steamed summer squash in a bit of water and added butter and brown sugar to make a squishy candy-coated vegetable that was one of the very few things she cooked that I didn't like. But making her squash with sorghum and spice makes everything nice.

This is best made with the small tender squash available early in the season. You can mix pattypans/cymlings, finger-sized yellow crook-necks or zucchini, or even mirilton/chayotes, if their skins are still very tender.

You can get the smoky bacon flavor either by adding 1 teaspoon of bacon drippings to the sauté oil, as recommended here, or ¼ teaspoon smoked Spanish paprika to the salt, if you want a meatless dish.

1 tablespoon sorghum syrup

⅛ teaspoon ground coriander

⅛ teaspoon ground cumin

⅛ teaspoon New Mexico red chile or cayenne

1 teaspoon bacon drippings

1 tablespoon olive oil

1 cup chopped sweet onion

4 generous cups summer squash, cubed thumbnail size

½ teaspoon salt

¼ teaspoon smoked Spanish paprika (optional)

In a small bowl or saucer, combine sorghum, coriander, cumin, and red chile until blended. Set aside.

In a wide skillet over medium heat, melt bacon drippings and heat oil. (If you forgo the bacon drippings, increase the oil by 1 teaspoon.) Add onions and sauté until just beginning to soften. Add squash to skillet and toss to coat with oil. (If you are not using bacon drippings, mix salt and paprika.) Season with the salt and mix well. Turn heat very low and cover tightly. Let steam for 3 minutes, until squash is beginning to get tender in the center but skin still has resilience.

Remove cover and turn heat up so liquid begins to bubble. Add sorghum mixture to the skillet, stirring and cooking for about 2 minutes or until the liquid is reduced to a very thin glaze. Remove from heat and let stand for a few minutes before serving. Serves 4 as a generous side dish.

Cinnamon Carrots

1 pound carrots
2 tablespoons butter
2 tablespoons sorghum syrup
1 tablespoon Orange Sorghum Vinegar (page 56)
⅛ teaspoon cinnamon
⅛ teaspoon salt

Peel carrots, trim, and cut into coins ½-inch thick. Place carrots in a saucepan with just enough water to cover. Bring to a quick boil, then turn heat to simmer, cover, and cook for 5 minutes, until just tender. Drain in colander.

Melt the butter in the saucepan over low heat, then add sorghum, vinegar, cinnamon, and salt and stir until blended. Add the carrots and increase heat to medium. Cook, stirring, to set glaze, about 5 minutes. Serve immediately. Serves 4 as side dish.

Fried Apples

My mama made fried apples with brown sugar, a lovely sweet side. Sorghum is more subtle and lets the flavor of the apples shine. Choose apples that have some tartness and that are not mushy for best results. Fried apples are a perfect side with any braised meat and just about all pork dishes. You can mix in a generous spoonful to sweeten a cup of Greek yogurt. And they can be spiked, or not, to become the topping for Kentucky Cakes 2.0 (page 70).

4 medium apples
1 tablespoon bacon drippings or butter
2 tablespoons sorghum syrup, divided

Quarter apples and remove core. If you're using the apples as a side dish, slice about ⅛-inch thick the long way. If you plan to use them as a topping for pancakes, slice them the short way.

In a skillet or sauté pan with lid, melt drippings over medium heat. Add the apples and lightly toss to coat. Cover and let sweat for 4 minutes. Remove lid and drizzle 1 tablespoon of sorghum on apples and lightly toss again to coat. Continue cooking uncovered for another minute or so until apples are tender and juice has been absorbed to make a light glaze. Set pan aside to let apples rest for a few minutes before serving. Pour 1 tablespoon of sorghum over apples and toss just before dishing up. Serves 4 as side dish.

Grilled Carolina Peaches with Sorghum Glaze

When I told my daughter and son-in-law I had this recipe from Lucky 32 in Greensboro, North Carolina, they were gobsmacked. "I could have made a whole meal just on that," Todd said. Executive Chef Jay Pierce weaves the sweet and salty here in fine style. You don't have to come to the Carolinas for your peaches (although you'd be glad if you did). Just buy fresh ripe ones from your local farmers market at the height of the season. Huge grocery peaches rarely deliver as much flavor. The portion size here is based on peaches about the size of a tennis ball. This is the perfect dessert for summer grilling because you can put the peaches over the still-warm coals.

For each person:

1½ peaches
3 tablespoons goat chèvre
3 very thin slices of country ham or *jamón serrano*
2 tablespoons Lucky Sorghum Glaze (page 58)

Peel peaches. (Immersing them in boiling water for 30 seconds then plunging them in an ice-water bath will loosen the skins considerably.) Halve peaches and discard pits. Place 1 tablespoon of chèvre into the cavity of each half. Wrap with ham, taking care to cover the cheese completely. Grill over low heat until ham is crispy and peach is warm through. Place on serving plate and drizzle with glaze.

Pear and Dried Cranberry Chutney

An earthy sweet hot condiment perfect for late-autumn winter meals when pears are in season. This is called for in the recipe for Curried Pumpkin Soup on page 75. It's also great for the time-honored southern hostess trick of serving crackers with a block of cream cheese covered with something sweet, hot, spicy, and fruity on top!

¾ pound Bosc or Anjou pears
Juice of 1 lime
½ cup cider vinegar
⅓ cup sorghum syrup
½ cup dried cranberries
½ tablespoon minced fresh ginger
½ teaspoon salt
¼ teaspoon ground coriander
¼ teaspoon ground cloves
⅛ teaspoon cayenne
1 teaspoon minced garlic

Quarter and core pears, but do not peel. Cut them into roughly ½-inch chunks and place in a bowl. Toss in lime juice and set aside.

In a nonaluminum pot, bring vinegar and sorghum to a boil over high heat, stirring until sorghum dissolves. Add the pears and remaining ingredients except garlic. When mixture boils again, turn heat to low and simmer for 30 minutes, uncovered, to thicken. Stir several times during the process to be sure mixture doesn't stick. Remove from heat and allow to cool, then transfer to lidded glass jars. This recipe should yield about 2 pints, and you can keep it, tightly covered, in the refrigerator for 2 to 3 weeks.

Main Events

Almost Nancie's Beef with Broccoli

Two of my favorite Asian cookbooks are Nancie McDermott's *Quick and Easy Thai* and *Quick and Easy Chinese*. I love them because the recipes are direct, clear, and simple but unfailingly produce scrumptious food. I also love them because my daughter and son-in-law own them, love to cook from them, and often feed me. As I was sighing over beef with broccoli one night, Meghan said to me, "You know I put sorghum in that." I didn't, because it's not flavor forward, but again, it works magic in weaving the harmony of the other flavors. So with thanks to Nancie, here's the Lundy-Jones adaptation.

¼ cup chicken stock
2 tablespoons oyster sauce
1 tablespoon tamari
1 teaspoon sorghum syrup
2 tablespoons water
2 teaspoons cornstarch
2 tablespoons vegetable oil
2 teaspoons chopped garlic
2 teaspoons chopped fresh ginger
½ pound thinly sliced beef
3 cups broccoli florets

In a medium bowl, combine the chicken stock, oyster sauce, tamari, and sorghum. Stir to make a smooth sauce. In a small bowl, combine water and cornstarch.

Heat a wok or large, deep skillet on high heat, and add the oil and swirl to coat the pan. Add the garlic and ginger and toss until they release their fragrance. Add the beef, spreading it out in a single layer. Cook undisturbed until the edges just change color (about 30 seconds) and then toss well. Add the broccoli florets and cook 1 minute, tossing once, until they are shiny and bright green.

Add the chicken stock mixture by pouring it around the sides of the pan. Cook, tossing often, until the broccoli is tender and the beef is done, about 2 to 3 minutes.

Add the cornstarch mixture to the center of the pan. Toss to combine everything well, and as soon as the sauce thickens, transfer to a serving plate. Serve hot or warm with steamed rice. Serves 4.

Citrus Sorghum Asian Noodles

Cold Asian noodles are a staple of the health food deli case and are often made with sesame seed paste. Peanut butter gives a deeper, richer taste that works beautifully with sorghum and a citrusy vinegar. The resulting fresh and fruity sauce lends itself to new garnishes, as well: fennel instead of cucumbers, sweet Vidalia onions instead of green, carrots, and a splash of sunny orange.

This recipe makes enough for a vegetarian meal for two or an appetizer for more. It also makes a tantalizing side for Mary to Martha to Me Sesame Sorghum Pork Chops (page 113).

PEANUT SAUCE

3 tablespoons peanut butter

2 tablespoons tamari

2 tablespoons hot water

1 tablespoon sorghum syrup

1 teaspoon fresh tart orange juice

1 teaspoon rice vinegar

1 teaspoon chile garlic paste, or to taste

In a bowl large enough to toss noodles and additional ingredients below, combine above ingredients and whisk to make a creamy sauce.

NOODLES

8 ounces fresh Chinese noodles or spaghetti
Salt
½ cup slivered fresh fennel root
Supremes from 1 small orange
¼ cup chopped Vidalia onion
2 carrots, grated

Cook noodles in a large pot of boiling, salted water. When al dente, drain well and transfer to bowl with sauce. Toss to coat. Taste, and add salt if needed.

Add the fennel, orange supremes, onion, and carrots and toss well to distribute evenly. May be served immediately or chilled to serve later.

Red Thai Curry

Feel free to experiment with other meats or vegetables in this flexible, delectable recipe. And if you want to go vegetarian, use chick-peas for the chicken. You can also add a couple of handfuls of fresh spinach when you add the chicken.

1 medium-sized butternut squash or large sweet potato
1 (14- to 15-ounce) can coconut milk, divided
1 to 2 tablespoons red curry paste, or to taste
¾ cup reduced-sodium chicken broth or water
2 tablespoons fish sauce
1 tablespoon sorghum syrup
¾ pound boneless chicken meat, cut into small cubes
½ cup coarsely chopped fresh basil or cilantro
3 cups hot cooked rice

Peel, seed, and dice the butternut squash into ½- to ¾-inch cubes. Set aside.

In a wide, heavy skillet over high heat, warm about half the coconut milk, stirring frequently, for 2 to 3 minutes, until thickened and reduced by half. Add curry paste, and cook 2 minutes, stirring to mix into the coconut milk. Add remaining coconut milk, broth, fish sauce, sorghum, and butternut squash. Bring to a boil, reduce heat, and cook 30 minutes, or until squash is soft. Stir in chicken cubes and cook 5 minutes more. Remove from heat, stir in basil. Serve over rice. Serves 4.

Jazzy Jerry's Rice and Shrimp

My friend Jerry Kerr lives in Santa Fe these days but grew up in Baltimore and so gets a craving for seafood in the high desert. He's perfected a basic shrimp and rice recipe that he urges friends to riff on. This is my rendition in his and the Old Bay's honor.

Jerry suggests you remove shrimp shells and the dark "vein" before cooking, but I'm used to eating with southerners who don't mind a little peeling at the table. Choose whichever works best for you.

1½ pounds 21/25 shrimp in shells
1 (14.5-ounce) can fire-roasted tomatoes
3 cloves garlic, chopped
¼ cup chopped onion
¼ cup sorghum syrup
½ tablespoon Old Bay Seasoning
1 teaspoon ground New Mexico red chile powder or cayenne
1 tablespoon sea salt
1 tablespoon olive oil
1½ cups Basmati rice
1 cup fresh or frozen baby lima beans
2 cups chicken broth
1 cup fresh or frozen shoepeg corn

Rinse shrimp (if peeling and removing vein, do so now), then set aside in refrigerator.

Put tomatoes, garlic, onion, sorghum, Old Bay Seasoning, chile, and salt in blender or processor and purée.

Add oil to a deep skillet or wide pot with lid and warm on medium heat. Add the rice and stir to coat and toast just a bit. Add the tomato mixture and stir until it begins to bubble. Turn heat to low, stir in lima beans, cover, and cook at a low simmer for 10 minutes.

While rice is cooking, warm chicken broth in microwave or on stove until steaming. When the rice has finished simmering for 10 minutes, add the chicken broth and corn. Stir, cover, and cook for 15 minutes, occasionally stirring to prevent sticking.

Taste to see if rice is tender, and if not, cook a little longer. When rice is tender, nestle shrimp on top, cover, and simmer for 5 minutes. Shrimp are cooked when they turn pink; don't overcook. Serve immediately. Serves 6.

Sorghum-Glazed Fennel Salmon

I have a small hand spice grinder and use it to barely grind the fennel seeds. You can use a mortar and pestle as well. The idea is to release the flavor but not create a powder. Fennel that is sold already ground has lost a good bit of the brightness that is part of its appeal. This salmon pairs beautifully with Arugula Fennel Citrus Salad (page 78), and you can reserve some of the fennel fronds from that recipe to garnish the salmon prettily.

½ tablespoon fennel seed, ground
½ tablespoon coarse salt
¼ teaspoon freshly ground black pepper
4 salmon fillets (about 6 ounces each), with skin
Olive oil
Lucky Sorghum Glaze (page 58)

Combine fennel, salt, and pepper. Rub into the surface of the skin-less side of the salmon.

In a nonstick skillet over medium, heat the oil until just glistening. Lay fillets, skin-side down, in the oil, turn heat to high, and cook for three minutes. Use a thin spatula to gently flip, then turn heat to medium and cook for 5 minutes more, until flesh is firm and pink in the middle. Place on plates with seasoned side up and drizzle with glaze. Serve immediately. Serves 4.

Sticky Fingers Chesapeake Bay Red Crabs

This crab feast is for the fearless who don't mind cracking crabs and licking fingers as they go. Best made with Chesapeake Bay red crabs, but if you can't get them where you are, well, we won't tell. Chef Travis Milton of Comfort in Richmond, Virginia, came up with this delight. I lift my cold pale ale in sticky fingers to salute him.

3 gallons water
¼ cup salt
1 dozen live Chesapeake Bay red or blue crabs
Ice water
½ tablespoon butter
2 medium shallots, finely minced
1 clove garlic, finely minced
1½ teaspoons red pepper flakes
2 teaspoons lime juice
1 teaspoon apple cider vinegar
3 cups sorghum syrup
3 tablespoons chopped fresh cilantro

In a large stock pot on high heat, bring water and salt to a boil. Turn heat down until it's at a lively simmer, put crabs in the pot, and cook for 6 minutes. Remove and shock with ice water to stop cooking, then drain.

Use a crab cracker to gently crack the legs and sides of shells, and rinse away any broken shell pieces. Place in a very large mixing bowl, such as a bread bowl.

In a small sauté pan on medium heat, melt butter. Add shallots and garlic and sauté until the garlic just turns golden. Add the red pepper flakes and toast for 30 seconds.

Deglaze the pan with lime juice and vinegar (this is pungent, so don't stand right over the pan). Add the sorghum, stirring as you do. Turn the heat lower and continue to stir; let the mixture reduce by a quarter.

Pour warm sorghum mixture over the crabs and toss briefly. Sprinkle chopped cilantro and toss until crabs are evenly coated in syrup and cilantro. Transfer to platter and serve with cold beer and paper towels. Serves 4.

Miso-Sorghum Chicken with Kale

My good friend and cookbook author Sarah Fritschner worked some alchemy with the ingredients here, and the result is a magical mélange. You can make fried rice with the leftovers—if you have any!

2 tablespoons vegetable oil
2 medium onions, chopped
1 tablespoon finely chopped peeled ginger
1 tablespoon finely chopped garlic
⅓ cup bourbon
¼ cup dark miso
3 tablespoons sorghum syrup
½ teaspoon hot sauce or Chinese garlic chile paste
1 (1-pound) bag chopped kale
1 medium carrot
2 cups chicken broth or water
4 bone-in chicken thighs
Salt and black pepper
4 cups cooked white rice

Heat oven to 350°F.

Heat vegetable oil in a wide, heavy skillet over medium-high heat. Add onions and cook until softened and beginning to brown, 15 minutes or more. Stir often and reduce heat as necessary. Add ginger and garlic and cook 10 minutes more. The mixture should be greatly reduced, darker and soft. Increase heat to high, add bourbon, and bring to a boil, scraping up bits from the bottom of the pan as you do. Remove from heat and stir in miso, sorghum, and hot sauce. You may need to mash the miso to blend it in.

Put kale in a 9-by-13-inch baking dish, pressing down to sort of cram it in. The pan will be over full. Peel and trim the carrot, slice it in fourths lengthwise, and cut in 1-inch lengths; sprinkle them over the kale. Dollop the onion mixture over the kale and pour in broth or water. Put chicken pieces on the kale, sprinkle with salt and pepper, and cover the dish with heavy-duty aluminum foil, crimping tightly. Bake chicken for 30 minutes, remove the foil, and bake 30 minutes more. Serve kale and chicken with cooked white rice. Serves 4.

Chicken Yassa Style

The remarkable Jessica Harris, African-food scholar, taught me the right way to make the Senegalese favorite, chicken yassa, and her version is delicious. But that was over twenty years ago, and as beloved recipes often do, this one has changed to fit the needs of my diet, the preferences of my taste, and the likely contents of my larder. In that two decade journey, I've never made a version I didn't like. The combination of tangy lemon, pungent onion, and fiery pepper in the marinade is almost perfect—it only needed sorghum syrup to bring it all together in bliss. Senegalese chicken yassa is served on rice to soak up the juices, but you might want to try it with a hot skillet of Real Cornbread (page 64) to sop.

The chicken needs to marinate, refrigerated, for at least 3 hours, and can do so overnight.

3 lemons (juicy, with thin skins)
1½ tablespoons sorghum syrup

2 tablespoons chopped roasted New Mexico green chile (or other hot pepper you prefer)

½ tablespoon toasted sesame oil

1 teaspoon salt

½ teaspoon black pepper

4 medium onions

3½ pounds chicken leg quarters

1 tablespoon peanut oil or other oil

½ cup water

Zest the lemons until you have ½ tablespoon, then juice. Combine in a bowl with sorghum and stir until dissolved. Mix in chile, sesame oil, salt, and pepper.

Halve onions and slice in rounds about ¼-inch thick. Place onions, marinade, and chicken pieces in a large plastic freezer bag, press out air, and seal, then shake and move around until chicken and onions are mixed together and coated in the marinade. Place in refrigerator for at least 3 hours, turning the bag at least once to make sure marinade coats everything equally. If you marinate overnight, turn a few more times.

When you are ready to cook, turn on broiler. Remove chicken from bag, shaking off any clingy onions, and lay in one layer on broiler rack. Broil on each side until lightly browned. Be careful not to burn. You can also brown on a grill.

Heat oil in the bottom of a Dutch oven or wide, heavy pan with lid. Remove onions from marinade, shaking lightly in the bag to drain a bit. (You can use finger or tongs, but I find one of those clawlike pasta scoopers works very well.) Add onions to oil, being careful not to get burned, as the oil will pop when drops of marinade hit it. Sauté onions in the oil until they soften and just begin to turn golden.

Add the marinade to the pot along with water and bring to a boil. Add the chicken in one layer, if possible. (If you have to layer a few pieces on top, move then around with a spoon during cooking to make sure all pieces come in contact with the hot marinade.) Cover the pot, turn heat to a low simmer, and cook for 35 minutes, until chicken is tender. Serves 4.

Monkey Wrench Skillet Fried Chicken

Here's what Louisville, Kentucky, restaurant reviewer Marty Rosen has to say about the fried chicken at Dennie Humphrey's artful eatery and performance space, the Monkey Wrench: "It's a plate that stays true to its southern origins but blends the tradition with keenly imaginative touches: the rich dark sweetness of local sorghum, hints of smoke, a dash of heat supplied by a fire-roasted banana pepper aioli."

Here's how Executive Chef Dustin Staggers pulls it off, adapted for the home cook. The first trick he uses is to soak the chicken overnight in brine made of the combined juice from pickled banana peppers and dill pickles. You do not need to be exact in making this brine at home. You want about a cup, and if you don't have quite enough, you can add salted water to extend (1 teaspoon salt to ¼ cup water). You will use some of the banana peppers for the aioli and can use others to garnish.

CHICKEN

4 large chicken breasts with skin and bone
½ cup juice from jar of pickled banana peppers, plus more if needed
½ cup juice from jar of dill pickles, plus more if needed
½ cup flour
½ teaspoon salt
¼ teaspoon freshly ground pepper
4 tablespoons melted butter (optional)
Lard or vegetable shortening to fry
2 tablespoons sorghum syrup
Banana Pepper Aioli (see below)

Marinate the chicken for 24 hours in brine made from combining the juice from pickled banana peppers and juice from dill pickles in a large, sealable, plastic food-storage bag.

When you are ready to fry, in a separate plastic bag, combine the flour, salt, and pepper. Remove chicken and discard brine. (At the Monkey Wrench, cooks pat the chicken dry and dredge in melted butter, but you may skip this step if you wish.) Place chicken, one piece at a time, in the flour mixture, close bag, and shake and turn gently until chicken is evenly coated in the flour. As you remove the piece from the bag, shake gently to discard any loose breading. Do the same for each piece of chicken.

In a large skillet, preferably cast iron, melt enough lard or shortening to fill the skillet ½-inch deep. Turn the heat to high and adjust as necessary so that the grease is hot enough that a fleck of flour dances but not hot enough to smoke, about 350°F.

Lay the chicken in the hot oil, skin side down, then turn the heat to medium and fry until the skin side gets golden and crispy, 12 to 15 minutes. Turn chicken over, and fry until that side is golden as well and chicken reaches an internal temperature of 165°F. Remove to drain briefly on rack. Serve warm, crisscrossed with drizzles of sorghum and aioli. Serves 4.

BANANA PEPPER AIOLI

2 tablespoons minced pickled banana pepper
2 teaspoons juice from jar of pickled banana peppers
¼ cup mayonnaise
1 tablespoon sour cream, buttermilk, or plain Greek yogurt
Salt and black pepper

Combine all the ingredients, adding salt and pepper to taste.

Seared Steak and Lentil Salad

This savory but nourishing salad has become a favorite entrée served with a hearty bread.

1 cup dried green lentils
2 cups water
¾ teaspoon salt
1 tablespoon sorghum syrup

1 tablespoon soy sauce
3 tablespoons Orange Sorghum Vinegar (page 56), divided
1 pound skirt, Denver, or sirloin steak, about 1-inch thick, visible fat removed
1 head fennel sliced fine in 1-inch lengths
½ cup mayonnaise
2 tablespoons minced fresh fennel fronds
Salt and freshly ground black pepper

Pick over lentils, discarding any wrinkled ones or debris, then rinse and place in saucepan. Add water and bring to a lively simmer on high, then turn heat down to create a gentle simmer. Cook for 20 to 30 minutes uncovered, until lentils are just tender but still whole (al dente). Drain and place in large bowl, then add salt and toss.

While lentils are cooking, make the marinade by combining sorghum, soy sauce, and 1 tablespoon of the vinegar, stirring until sorghum is dissolved. Soak the steak in marinade at room temperature for 20 minutes, turning 3 or 4 times to equally dredge both sides.

Remove steak from marinade and let drain on rack while you heat the pan, but do not pat the steak dry. Choose a cast-iron or heavy steel skillet that will allow the steak to cover most of the surface. Spray the skillet lightly with cooking oil and heat on medium high until a few drops of water splashed on the surface skitter and dance. Lay steak on hot surface and leave for about two minutes to sear, then turn and brown the other side as well. Remove from pan to deglaze, using the marinade for liquid. Return steak to pan and simmer on medium for 3 to 5 minutes, turning once, until steak is cooked medium rare.

Remove pan from heat and steak from pan, and using a minimum of water (1 to 2 tablespoons), deglaze pan again and set aside. Slice meat in thin strips, then cut strips in bite-size pieces, about 1-inch wide. Pour warm marinade over the steak and toss to coat. Mix steak and marinade with the lentils. Add sliced fennel and toss.

In a small bowl, whisk together mayonnaise, 2 tablespoons of the vinegar, and minced fennel fronds. Pour over lentil and steak mixture and toss thoroughly to coat. Add salt and pepper to taste. Serves 6 as main course salad.

Slow-Cooked Chuck Feast

My local market sells boneless chuck steak in 3-pound packages, and I like to cook it all in a slow cooker and make two nights' meals out of it. For supper the first night I serve the slow-cooked meat over a nest of mashed potatoes or over split-open wedges of Real Cornbread (page 64). The next day I make beef stew with the remaining meat and pan juices. This mouth-watering meat can also be shredded when done to make French dip sandwiches for a game-day feast. The au jus will have you saying, "Aw, yeah!"

1 cup chopped bell pepper
1 cup chopped onion
3 pounds boneless chuck steak about 1-inch thick
2 teaspoons salt
½ teaspoon fresh cracked pepper
¼ teaspoon cinnamon
Oil to coat pan
1 cup white wine or apple cider
⅓ cup sorghum syrup
½ teaspoon celery seed
¼ teaspoon salt
⅛ teaspoon ground mustard
1 (14.5-ounce) can fire-roasted diced tomatoes

Lightly spray the interior of large slow cooker with oil. Mix pepper and onion and put about half in the bottom of the cooker.

Trim any large pieces of fat from the meat. Mix the salt, pepper, and cinnamon together and rub into the surface of the meat. Coat a heavy skillet with oil and brown the meat on both sides. Lay enough pieces in the cooker to just cover the onions and pepper; then spread remaining onions and pepper on top and lay the rest of the meat over that.

Deglaze the pan with white wine or cider on low heat and stir in sorghum to dissolve. Add the celery seed, salt, and ground mustard to the liquid, then the tomatoes. Stir until just heated. Pour over the meat, cover with lid, and set cooker on high. Cook for 4 hours. Meat will be extremely tender and fall into large chunks. Serve as described above with a ladleful of "gravy."

This quantity can serve up to 8 people, but I prefer to make it a meal for 4 and make stew the next day.

To make stew: Refrigerate the remaining meat and pan juices separately. When you are ready to prepare, chop 2 unpeeled medium potatoes and 6 peeled carrots into bite-sized chunks. Place in a stew pot and cover with the pan juices. If you need additional liquid, you can add beef or vegetable broth or wine, but it's usually enough. Cover and cook on medium for about 20 minutes until vegetables are very tender. Add the meat and serve. This makes enough for 4 generous portions.

Kentucky Lamb Shoulder

Kentucky was famous for the lamb raised there in the first part of the twentieth century, but most of it was shipped out of state since few locals ate it back then. That story has changed in recent years as small sustainable and delectable lamb operations have become an integral part of the flourishing local farm-to-table scene. One of that scene's greatest supporters is Louisville's Sarah Fritschner, who has for more than two decades now devoted her time and energy to making connections between the folks who cook and those who grow. This is one of her many recipes highlighting the best of the bluegrass.

3 pounds lamb shoulder
Salt and black pepper
¼ cup olive oil, divided
1 cup chopped onion
1 rib celery, chopped
3 to 5 large garlic cloves, minced
1 teaspoon thyme leaves
1 teaspoon fennel seed
½ teaspoon red pepper flakes

3 cups chicken stock or reduced-sodium chicken broth
1 cup bourbon
¼ cup sorghum syrup
1 tablespoon vinegar

Trim the meat of outside fat. Pat meat dry and season with salt and ¼ teaspoon pepper. Heat 2 tablespoons of the oil in a 5-quart heavy pot over medium-high heat until it shimmers. Brown meat well on both sides and remove to a dish. Add the remaining 2 tablespoons of oil to pot, then add onion and celery, and cook over medium-high heat for 10 minutes, stirring occasionally. Add garlic and cook, stirring, 10 minutes more, lowering the heat if vegetables begin sticking. The onions should have reduced quite a bit and be very tender.

Add thyme, fennel seed, red pepper flakes, and ½ teaspoon black pepper to the pan. Return meat to pot and add stock, bourbon, sorghum, and vinegar. Reduce heat to low and simmer, covered, stirring occasionally, until meat is very tender. This should take 3 to 3½ hours. (If you would prefer, you may transfer meat to a slow cooker and cook on low heat for 8 hours or more.)

Remove meat from sauce and discard bones and any obvious fat. Cover and chill meat and sauce separately. To serve, discard any fat from the top of the sauce and reheat meat and sauce together until warm through (on top of the stove or in an oven preheated to 350°F, covered, for 30 minutes or so). Serves 6.

Mary to Martha to Me Sesame Sorghum Pork Chops

My friend Martha's friend Mary cooks pork tenderloin with a honey sesame glaze. She gave the recipe to Martha, who decided to make a marinade. Martha gave the recipe to me, and I upped the marinade ingredients and dropped the pork loin for chops. Now it's your turn.

¼ cup plus 1 tablespoon sorghum syrup, divided
¼ cup tamari

3 tablespoons Orange Sorghum Vinegar (page 56)
2 tablespoons toasted sesame oil
1 clove garlic, minced
4 pork chops, about ¾-inch thick with bone in and some fat
    around the edges
¼ cup sesame seeds, divided

In a bowl, combine 1 tablespoon of the sorghum, tamari, vinegar, sesame oil, and garlic, whisking until sorghum is dissolved. Pour into a Ziploc bag large enough to hold the pork chops. Add the chops, seal the bag, gently pushing out air as you do, and then turn and slosh things around in the bag until all chops are coated. Refrigerate for 4 hours, turning at least once to make sure marinade is evenly distributed.

When you are ready to bake, heat oven to 375°F. Oil a rack and place it on a baking sheet lined with foil.

Remove chops from bag and discard marinade. Lay chops on rack and drizzle lightly with no more than half of the remaining sorghum, less if warranted. (You do not want a thick glaze but just a light sheen to help the sesame seeds adhere and give an undercurrent of flavor.) Sprinkle half of the sesame seeds over chops and pat lightly to adhere. Turn over and coat the second side of each chop with the remaining sorghum and sesame seeds. Bake chops for 20 minutes, turn with tongs, and bake for an additional 15 minutes, or until done (see note). Allow to rest 5 minutes and then serve. Serves 4.

Note: Most restaurants these days cook chops to an internal temperature of 145°F as registered by a meat thermometer, then let them rest for 5 minutes so that the heat rises. The USDA agrees this is safe practice, and many prefer the pink chop that results. I admit I'm not one, and so I cook my chops until the thermometer registers 155°F or so.

Pork Pot with Sweet Potatoes and Beans

3 pounds country-style pork ribs
Salt and black pepper
1 tablespoon olive oil
1 cup water
2 tablespoons sorghum syrup
1 tablespoon Dijon-style mustard
½ teaspoon salt
1 pound sweet potatoes, cut in ¾-inch-wide rounds
1 large onion, cut in chunks and layers separated
2 (15-ounce) cans cannellini beans

Heat oven to 350°F.

Trim excess fat from ribs, if necessary. Salt and pepper lightly.

In a Dutch-oven-style pot that can go in the oven, brown ribs in olive oil on medium heat, removing from pot when they are browned on both sides. Pour off grease and deglaze the pan with water. Remove from heat and add sorghum, mustard, and salt, stirring to blend.

Layer sweet potato rounds, onions, and beans alternately in the liquid in pot. Lay the ribs over the top. Place on burner on high and bring liquid just to a boil. Remove from heat.

Cover and place pot in oven and bake for 1 hour. Remove cover and bake an additional 30 minutes. To serve, remove ribs and spoon the sweet potato mixture into wide plates. Place ribs on top or to the side. Serves 6.

Sweet Potato Hash

I'm repeating a recipe here from *Butter Beans to Blackberries*, because it's just too good not to. The sorghum syrup is what marries the sweet and salty and will make you use your biscuit to sop up every drop.

6-ounce slice country ham
1 cup warm water
1 tablespoon sorghum syrup
4–5 drops Tabasco
4 cups peeled and diced sweet potato
1 cup finely chopped onion

To render drippings for the hash, fry the ham in a hot skillet on both sides until some browning occurs. Remove from heat and remove the ham to a plate and trim the fat. Return the fat to the skillet and fry for 2 to 3 minutes, pressing with the back of a metal spatula to extract as much grease as possible. Remove and discard the fat.

Turn heat to medium. Gently, down the side of the skillet, pour the warm water into the pan and deglaze. Add the sorghum and stir to dissolve. Add the Tabasco and sweet potatoes. Cover and simmer for 5 minutes.

Chop the ham into ½-inch dice while the potatoes are simmering. When 5 minutes are up, add the ham and onion. Simmer, covered, for 5 more minutes. Serve immediately, or if you wish to top with fried or poached eggs, you can remove from heat and leave covered while you prepare the eggs. This is delicious served over Ouita's Biscuits (page 63) or side by side with steaming grits.

Red Chile Cheese Enchiladas with Eggs

Enchilada means "in chile" and what makes an enchilada that is dredging the corn tortillas in the chile sauce before assembling, not pouring it on after. (Although you are always welcome to add a little more after the dredge and assembly.)

In much of the United States, most restaurants serve enchiladas as cylinders rolled around whatever filling you have requested. The enchiladas you get in New Mexico and parts of Arizona are more likely to be flat or stacked. I prefer the taste and texture of the multilayered flat tortillas, and they are way easier to work with. You simply assemble them on an oven-proof plate as described below, run them under the broiler to melt the top cheese, and eat.

This can be consumed for breakfast but is not exclusively a breakfast dish. Traditionally tortillas are lightly fried in hot oil to soften, but I've been making this for years without that step and it tastes delightful.

For each person served:

⅓ cup New Mexico Red Chile Sauce (page 59)
3 corn tortillas
½ cup finely grated Monterrey Jack cheese, divided
¼ cup finely chopped white onion, divided
1 egg, fried over easy

Turn on broiler to low and arrange rack directly below.

Have warm sauce ready and all other ingredients nearby. Dredge tortilla in sauce, submerging and lifting out quickly (use a flat spatula or your fingers, or both). You want it to be immersed but not saturated to the extent that it falls apart. Lay flat on oven-proof plate and spread ⅓ of the cheese evenly on top, then sprinkle on ⅓ of the onion. Repeat. Do the same with the third tortilla, but this time put down the onions first and top with cheese. Place under the broiler and heat until top cheese melts and begins to turn brown. Serve with fried egg on top.

Note: Enchiladas are a great way to use up leftover meat. Red chile is exceptionally good with shredded pork, lamb, or beef. Beef from the Slow-Cooked Chuck Feast (page 111) can be used in place of the cheese in the filling in the recipe above. Top with cheese and brown in the broiler and serve with the egg, as well as a dollop of sour cream with minced fresh cilantro garnish. If you have leftovers from Kentucky Lamb Shoulder (page 112), do the same as for beef but top with Greek yogurt and minced fresh mint.

Drinks and Nibbles

Southern Lassi

I fell in love with lassi the first time I was served it at an Indian restaurant. Its tart, sweet, spicy dance is perfect for summer days and southern climes. Normally it's made with yogurt, but when I can find real buttermilk from a small dairy, that ups the divine, and sorghum syrup sends it over the top.

I like lassi at room temperature but realize that many do not. If you want your lassi cold, use frozen peaches. I also make this with a ripe banana.

---

1 cup buttermilk or yogurt
1 cup frozen or fresh peach chunks
1 tablespoon sorghum syrup
¼ teaspoon ground cinnamon
¼ teaspoon ground ginger

Place all ingredients in the blender and process until smooth. Serves 1.

Splendid Chai

This sweet hot tea from India simply warms the soul. It's nice with honey, but it's splendid with sorghum.

12 dime-size slices fresh ginger, halved
Seeds from 5 whole cardamom pods
1 cinnamon stick, broken
1 teaspoon fennel seed
½ teaspoon whole mixed peppercorns
6 whole cloves
4 cups water
2 tablespoons black leaf tea
1 cup whole milk
¼ cup sorghum syrup

Place all the spices in a heavy saucepan with the water. Bring to a boil, then turn down heat, cover snugly, and cook at a lively simmer for five minutes. Add black tea, cover, and simmer for 5 minutes more.

Add milk, and lower heat sufficiently so the mixture is steaming but not bubbling. Cover, remove from heat, and allow to steep for 5 minutes.

Strain into warmed teapot, add sorghum, and stir to dissolve. Serve immediately.

Note: This chai can also be refrigerated and consumed over ice as a refreshing summer beverage, or it may be made into a smoothie with a frozen chopped banana blended with 8 ounces of the chai mixture.

Spruce Beer, aka Pine/Apple Punch

Shortly before he opened Rhubarb in Asheville, North Carolina, John Fleer was walking past the bar when he noticed a jar of blackstrap molasses on one of the shelves. "Ah, no," he said to his head bartender, then went to the kitchen for a jug of Muddy Pond sweet sorghum syrup. "This is what we use around here." Not long after that, this party punch was born.

This recipe is for the flavorful syrup at the base of the drink. It makes 2½ quarts and can be stored up to two months in the refrigerator. When you are ready to prepare drinks, you'll need hard apple cider and soda as well. Combine 1 part syrup to 3 parts cider in a chilled mug and top with just enough soda to create a foamy head.

4½ cups water
1½ cups sorghum syrup
6 ounces dried juniper berries, mortared
2 ounces chopped sassafras root
4 tablespoons chopped fresh ginger
3 cups dark brown sugar

In a large pot over medium heat, combine all ingredients except sugar, and bring to a simmer, stirring occasionally. Simmer for 10 minutes, then gradually add sugar, stirring as you do. When sugar is dissolved, remove pot from heat and allow to cool. Strain and refrigerate until ready to use.

Anna's Sorghum Simple Syrup

Summit City Lounge owner Amelia Ruth Kirby said that when she opened her meeting, eating, and sipping establishment in 2007, one goal she had was that it "reflect the place where it is, the mountains of eastern Kentucky." Anna Bogle, who established an eclectic menu for both kitchen and bar, took that to heart.

"Mixing cocktails, I look for signifiers of this region," Anna says. "Sorghum is an obvious choice, a substitute for simple syrup, but it has a coffee flavor, so you use it where that is appropriate.

"The places where I would use sorghum are in almost all drinks that have a seasonal aspect to them—autumn or winter flavors. It pairs beautifully with bourbon, and with pears and apples. But I don't know that I have a specific rule of thumb."

She notes that two of the three cocktails she's invented and shared here, Fallen Apple (page 123) and Winter Pear (page 123), follow that train of thought, but the Sorgarita (page 124) was a wild card experiment that Amelia suggested, and as Anna fiddled with it, she discovered, "It works amazingly well. Makes me curious. Makes me want to experiment some more." In case you do, here's where to start.

1 cup sorghum syrup
½ cup boiling water

Mix sorghum and water well, then cool, and store covered in the refrigerator.

Fallen Apple

Anna Bogle said she wasn't exactly sure why she picked this name, but one sip of this fragrant heady potable and I knew exactly: It would have made Eve perfectly content to leave the Garden of Eden.

⅛ wedge of a medium-sized tart apple, like Granny Smith
1½ ounces good quality bourbon, such as Bulleit
1½ ounces Anna's Sorghum Simple Syrup (page 122)
Juice of half a lemon, strained
1½ ounces hard apple cider, such as Strongbow
Apple slice and cinnamon stick for garnish

Shake all ingredients except cider over ice. Double strain into a rocks glass over ice and top with cider. Garnish with an apple slice and a cinnamon stick.

Winter Pear

If the name of this cocktail suggests a delicate Japanese winter land-scape, one misted with snowflakes, well, that's just what it tastes like! Anna infused her own vodka with wild pears she found on a mountain hike. If you want to try your hand at it, there are numerous how-to guides online, but there are also plenty of good commercial pear vodkas available.

1 ounce pear vodka
1 ounce Anna's Sorghum Simple Syrup (page 122)
1 ounce half-and-half
1 teaspoon pear butter
2 barspoons (1 teaspoon) Amaro CioCiaro
Sorghum syrup and freshly grated nutmeg for garnish

Shake over ice. Double strain into a coupe glass. Garnish with a swirl of sorghum and a grating of fresh nutmeg.

Sorgarita

I had a bad formative experience with tequila and usually find that just a hint can make me wince, but this fresh and earthy rendition set all those memories to rest.

2 ounces good quality *reposado* tequila
Juice of 1 lime
1 ounce Anna's Sorghum Simple Syrup (page 122)
½ ounce simple syrup
3 to 5 drops habanero tincture (see note)
1 wedge of lime, for garnish

Shake and pour over ice in a tall glass. Garnish with a wedge of lime.

Note: Tinctures are intense infusions used in tiny amounts to make a big difference. To store and use yours, you'll want a small apothecary bottle with a dropper. To make a habanero tincture, slice 2 medium habanero peppers, place in a small glass jar, cover with 2 ounces of good-quality mescal, and allow to sit overnight. (If you like it hotter, let it sit longer.) Remove peppers and strain (to catch seeds) into a funnel fitted in the small apothecary jar. Cap and store in the refrigerator.

Sriracha Sorghum Wings

Sweet, hot, and irresistible, these spicy wings should be served with Buttermilk Sorghum Dressing (page 83) on the side for dipping and with strips of fresh celery or raw fennel for crunch. You can put a bottle of Sriracha on the table for some who like it hot and a plastic ketchup-type squeeze bottle of sorghum for those who want to amp up the sweetness level.

Wings benefit from brining first, making them juicier inside and crisper out.

WINGS

1 gallon water
½ cup salt

½ cup sorghum syrup

½ cup sugar

2 pounds chicken wings, disjointed and wing tips discarded

2 tablespoons coconut oil

2 tablespoons butter, melted

3 tablespoons minced garlic

1 teaspoon salt

½ teaspoon black pepper

SAUCE

⅓ cup sorghum syrup

¼ cup Sriracha

1 tablespoon tamari

2 teaspoons fresh lemon juice

To brine, place water in a large pot, add salt, sorghum, and sugar, and stir to dissolve. Submerge wings, cover, and place in refrigerator for 40 minutes.

When time is up, heat oven to 400°F. Spray a large, rimmed baking sheet with oil. Drain wings in colander and then pat dry with paper towels. Place in a large bowl.

In a small bowl, whisk together the coconut oil, butter, garlic, salt, and pepper. Pour over the wings and toss well to coat. Lay wings on baking sheet in a single layer with a little space between wings.

Bake for 45 minutes to 1 hour, until browned and crisp, Use tongs and turn once during the process. Near the end of the baking time, make sauce.

To make sauce, mix sorghum, Sriracha, tamari, and lemon juice until fully blended.

When wings are browned and crisp, transfer to a big bowl and pour sauce over them, tossing very gently to coat. Transfer to a warm platter, drizzle any sauce remaining in bowl over them, and serve immediately. Serves 4 as an appetizer.

Potted Chicken Livers

Sharp-dressed, blues-playing Chef Colin Perry hails from Whitley City, Kentucky, so he pulls a couple of homeboy secrets from his arsenal when making this velvety chicken liver paste at Montreal's Dinette Triple Crown. A little bourbon here, a bit of sorghum there, a dash of Tabasco, and the crowd murmurs, "*Mmmmm, très bon.*"

1 pound trimmed chicken livers
3 teaspoons kosher or fine sea salt
Oil for cooking
⅔ cup minced shallots
1½ tablespoons minced garlic
1 teaspoon fresh thyme leaves
¼ cup bourbon
½ teaspoon black pepper
1 teaspoon Worcestershire sauce
1 teaspoon Tabasco
2 tablespoons sorghum syrup
7 tablespoons butter, chilled
7 tablespoons bacon fat, chilled, plus more for storage

Place a heavy skillet (preferably cast iron) on high to heat. While it's heating, toss the chicken livers with salt in a medium bowl until evenly seasoned.

When skillet is hot, add a thin layer of oil, and then add the chicken livers with enough space between so they are not touching. Cook for 2 to 3 minutes on each side until lightly browned on both but livers are still pink in the center. Cook in batches, placing cooked livers in a clean bowl as you go. If necessary, adjust the heat as you cook so the skillet doesn't get too hot and burn.

When livers are done, pour off any excess oil, and then add shallots. Stir with a wooden spoon, scraping browned bits from the bottom of the pan as you do. When the shallots begin to cook, add the garlic and thyme, and allow to soften. Add the bourbon and reduce until mixture is almost dry.

Place the livers, shallot mixture, pepper, Worcestershire sauce, Tabasco, and sorghum in a food processor and, while adding butter and bacon fat a little at a time, process until smooth. Taste and adjust seasoning, if needed, keeping in mind that this will be served chilled and so it should be slightly overseasoned while warm.

Pass mixture through a fine mesh strainer and then pack into five 125-ml Mason jars, pouring a thin layer of bacon grease over the top to keep fresh. Cover and refrigerate for up to 2 weeks. Serve with small sweet gherkins and toast or crackers.

Spicy Sorghum-Glazed Pecans

My good friend and great cookbook author Sheri Castle offered to develop this recipe for me, and when it was done, she wrote a note that virtually sighed with delight. They are good!

---

1 tablespoon butter, melted

3 tablespoons sorghum syrup

¾ teaspoon coarse salt

¼ teaspoon freshly ground black pepper

¼ teaspoon ground cinnamon

⅛ teaspoon cayenne

1½ cups pecan halves

2 tablespoons coarse, raw sugar

Heat oven to 325°F. Line a rimmed baking sheet with nonstick aluminum foil or parchment paper.

In a large bowl, stir together butter, sorghum, salt, black pepper, cinnamon, and cayenne until smooth. Add pecans and stir well to coat. Spread in single layer on baking sheet.

Bake 15 minutes, stirring every 5 minutes, until pecans are deeply toasted and the glaze gently bubbles. Remove from oven. Immediately sprinkle sugar over pecans and toss to coat.

Cool on the baking pan, separating any large clumps of nuts as soon as they are cool enough to touch. Glaze hardens as it cools.

Serve immediately or store in an airtight container at room temperature. Makes 2½ cups.

Warm Cinnamon Grapes with Sorghum Balsamic Glaze

Light spice and sorghum add an extra layer of warmth and mystery. These are the perfect accompaniment to a cheese plate. I also like to mix them into thick, creamy Greek yogurt, and they are a delicious garnish for chicken or other poultry.

1 pound seedless red grapes
2 teaspoons sorghum syrup
¼ teaspoon balsamic vinegar
Pinch of coarse sea salt
¼ teaspoon cinnamon

Heat oven to 400°F. Lightly spray cooking oil on a baking pan with an edge. Rinse and dry grapes and remove from stems. Lay on pan. Drizzle sorghum over grapes and roll around with your fingers to coat well. Bake for 20 minutes.

Remove grapes from oven and drizzle balsamic vinegar over them. Sprinkle very lightly with coarse sea salt. You're not aiming for a salty taste but just a hint. Sprinkle with cinnamon and lightly toss. Grapes are most flavorful at room temperature. Makes 2 cups.

Sorghum Caramel Popcorn

Chef Travis Milton of Comfort in Richmond, West Virginia, serves this sweetly savory popcorn as a tasty premeal treat, but I can make a meal of it on an evening with a crisp autumn apple, a wedge of cheese, and just a little bourbon, branch water back.

4 tablespoons butter
¼ cup bacon grease
1 cup dark brown sugar
¼ cup sorghum syrup
1 teaspoon salt
½ teaspoon baking soda
1 quart popped popcorn
2 tablespoons sorghum or sesame seeds

Heat oven to 275°F. Line a cookie sheet with Silpat and set aside.

In a 2-quart pot on medium heat, melt the butter and bacon grease. Stir in the sugar, sorghum syrup, and salt and continue to stir until dissolved. Use a candy thermometer to gauge the heat, and when it reaches 240°F, remove from heat and stir in baking soda.

Toss popcorn in the warm caramel mixture and turn out onto the Silpat-lined sheet, lightly spreading. Sprinkle seeds over the popcorn and place in oven. Bake for 30 minutes, stirring every 10. Allow to cool and then serve or store in a large glass or tin container with tight lid. Makes 1 quart.

Sweet Treats

Sorghum and Bourbon Pecan Pie

The taste and texture of corn syrup put me off the Holy Grail of Deep South piedom at an early age. Sorghum syrup and a tot of bourbon brought me back. Mercy, but this pie is good.

1 nine-inch pie crust
1½ cups pecan halves
Pinch of fine sea salt
4 tablespoons butter
½ cup sorghum syrup
¼ cup half-and-half
1 cup sugar
2 tablespoons white cornmeal
⅛ teaspoon salt
4 eggs
3 tablespoons bourbon

Heat oven to 325°F. Place crust in 9-inch pan and flute to make a raised edge.

To toast pecans, lightly spray cookie sheet with oil. Spread pecans in single layer and very lightly salt. (You're not aiming for salted nuts for snacking but just a whisper of salt—less than ⅛ teaspoon.)

Roast pecans in oven for 5 minutes, remove, and use a spatula to stir and flip the pecans. Put back in oven and roast for 5 more minutes. If pecans are just starting to brown and smell fragrant, they are ready; turn them out in a bowl. If not, you may need to roast them for 1 to 2 minutes more before turning out.

To make pie, turn heat up to 350°F.

In small pan, melt butter, stir in sorghum to blend. Remove from heat and add half-and-half. Set aside.

In a small bowl, blend sugar, cornmeal, and salt.

In a large bowl, whisk the eggs until yolks and whites are fully blended. Whisk in the sorghum mixture. Whisk in the sugar mixture. When all is blended, add the pecans and the bourbon and stir to incorporate. Pour into piecrust. Bake on the middle rack for 40–50 minutes, until the center is set. Remove and cool on rack before slicing. Serves 8.

Mocha Sorghum Shoofly Pie

Nobody riffs on a classic dessert better than the delightful Karen Barker. She adds hot coffee to this Pennsylvania Dutch favorite, and we use sweet sorghum syrup instead of the traditional molasses. For another incredible recipe from *Sweet Stuff: Karen Barker's American Desserts*, check out her Black Walnut Angel Food Cake with Sorghum Syrup on page 139.

1 nine-inch pie crust, baked blind (see note)

1 cup flour

½ cup brown sugar

6 tablespoons butter, lightly chilled

1 cup hot brewed coffee

1 teaspoon baking soda

½ cup corn syrup

½ cup sorghum syrup

½ teaspoon vanilla

½ teaspoon kosher salt

Powdered sugar for serving

Prepare pie crust as described in note below. When you remove the crust from the oven, turn the temperature down to 350°F.

While the crust is in the oven, prepare the pie filling. Combine the flour, brown sugar, and butter in a small bowl by rubbing with fingertips or using a pastry blender to create uniform crumbs. Set aside.

Pour the hot coffee into a mixing bowl and add the baking soda. Whisk in the corn syrup, sorghum, vanilla, and salt.

Sprinkle the crumb mixture evenly over the bottom surface of the crust. Gently pour the coffee mixture over the crumbs, being careful not to pour over the sides of the crust.

Bake at 350°F for 35 to 40 minutes. The filling will appear puffed and set when done. Remove and allow to cool, and then keep at room temperature for 8 to 10 hours. Can be made a day ahead. Sprinkle generously with powdered sugar before serving. Serves 8 to 10.

Note: Blind baking is the term used for partially baking the crust for a single-crust pie, ensuring a crisper bottom. To do this, make pie crust, roll out, and place in a 9-inch pan, fluting the edges. (Save any crust scraps.) Karen recommends chilling or preferably freezing the crust until it is firm. Preheat oven to 375°F, remove crust from freezer, and place a generous sheet of parchment paper or aluminum foil on the entire crust, making sure there's overhang all around for ease of removal. Fit it into the shell and then fill it with dried rice or beans or pie weights. Bake for approximately 20 minutes, until the edges just start to color and the bottom no longer looks raw. Remove the paper and weights and return to the oven for an additional 8 minutes. During this time, the crust may puff up, and you should very gently prick with a fork to release air. Check the shell several times during the process, pricking as needed. When the bottom is set and dry to the touch, remove. Karen cautions to be careful not to overbake, as that may cause the shell to crack. It should not brown but be light in appearance. Brush egg white on any holes from the pricking or small cracks. Large cracks or tears need to be repaired using the saved pastry crust scraps as filler. This is particularly important for pies with liquid fillings, like this one. Prepare the filling while the crust is blind baking and fill the crust immediately after removing, and repairing, if needed. It should still be quite warm when you return it, filled, to the oven to finish.

Whiskey Sour-ghum Pie

An intoxicating riff on the chess pie theme. If you want to make a lemon pie without the bourbon, reserve extra lemon juice.

---

1 nine-inch pie crust
1 lemon
4 tablespoons butter
½ cup sorghum syrup
¼ cup half-and-half
1 cup sugar
2 tablespoons cornmeal
⅛ teaspoon salt
4 eggs
1½ tablespoons bourbon
8 slices of orange

Heat oven to 375°F. Place crust in 9-inch pan and flute to make a raised edge.

Zest the rind of the lemon and mince fine. Juice remaining lemon and set aside 1½ tablespoons and zest.

In small pan, melt butter; stir in sorghum to blend. Remove from heat and add half-and-half. Set aside.

In a small bowl, blend sugar, cornmeal, and salt.

In a large bowl, whisk the eggs until yolks and whites are fully blended. Whisk in the sorghum mixture. Add the lemon juice and zest and bourbon. Whisk in the sugar mixture. Pour into piecrust and bake on middle rack for 15 minutes, then turn heat to 350°F and bake for 25 additional minutes, or until center is set. Allow to cool on rack before serving. Garnish each piece with a curled orange slice. Serves 8.

Emily's Howdy Pandowdy with Cornmeal Biscuit Top

I met Emily Hilliard by virtue of Pi(e) Day, a celebration she and her friend Kentuckian Lora Smith dreamed up to celebrate pi on March

14 by baking a multitude of pies to share with friends. Emily is a young folklorist, and her website, www.nothinginthehouse.com, is about all things pie, cobbler, and slump. When she heard I was on the look-out for a stellar sorghum pandowdy, she offered to immerse herself in peaches until she came up with the best. And, boy, did she ever. This delectable reminds me of the old saying, "makes your eyes light up and your tummy say 'howdy!'"

For the cornmeal biscuit top:

¾ cup flour
¼ cup cornmeal
1 tablespoon sugar
1½ teaspoons baking powder
¼ teaspoon salt
3 tablespoons unsalted butter
½ cup heavy cream or buttermilk
Turbinado sugar, for dusting

For the filling:

6 cups peaches, cut into ¼- to ½-inch wedges
1 teaspoon lemon juice
½ cup flour
⅔ cup sorghum syrup
¼ teaspoon zested peeled fresh ginger
¼ teaspoon salt

In a medium bowl, whisk together flour, cornmeal, sugar, baking powder, and salt. With a knife and fork or pastry cutter, cut in the butter until mixture resembles the consistency of cornmeal and peas. Add cream and stir gently to combine. Form dough into a ball, and cover in plastic wrap. Store in the refrigerator for at least 20 minutes while you prepare the filling.

Heat oven to 375°F. Lightly grease and flour the inside of a 9-inch cast-iron skillet, or if that is unavailable, a deep casserole dish of similar size.

In a medium bowl, combine peaches, lemon juice, flour, and sorghum. Stir in the ginger as well as the salt. Pour filling into the prepared skillet. Cover top with foil and bake for 25 minutes.

While filling is baking, roll out chilled biscuit dough on a clean, floured surface into a 9-to-10-inch circle. Cut 6 to 8 rounds with a biscuit cutter. Set aside.

Once filling has baked, remove from oven, and arrange cut biscuits evenly over the filling. Sprinkle with turbinado sugar. Return to the oven and bake for 20 to 25 minutes more, until biscuit dough is light golden and filling is bubbling.

Remove from the oven and spoon some of the steaming filling over the biscuit top and return to the oven to bake 5 to 10 minutes more. Remove from oven and let cool. Serve slightly warm.

Fried Pies

Little handheld pastries with sweet or savory fillings are ubiquitous the world over and many have curious names like pasties or empanadas. In the South, though, we just call them fried pies (even those that are nowadays sometimes baked). The ones I grew up eating were made with dried mountain apples; further south, folks dried the abundant peaches. That's what is featured here in honor of my friend Greg Johnson, who had this to say about why dried fruit beats fresh here:

> I like dried peaches in fried pies because drying intensifies their flavor. Drying wrings out all of the unessential information in the raw fruit, like what kind of summer it was or how hard it landed when it fell, until there's only one thing it has on its mind, which it will whisper languidly in your ear through plump, pursed lips: "peachhhhhhh." When you bite into a dried-peach fried pie, it's not just delicious. It's like Marilyn singing you "Happy Birthday."

2¼ cups flour, plus more for dusting

1 teaspoon kosher salt

½ teaspoon baking powder

¾ cup hot skim milk

½ cup lard or vegetable shortening, chilled and cut up

2 cups unsweetened dried peaches

2 cups water, plus more as needed

⅓ to ½ cup sorghum syrup

Lard or oil with high smoke point, for frying

In a medium bowl, mix the flour with the salt and baking powder. In a large bowl, combine the milk with the lard and stir until most of the lard is melted but there are a few pea-size pieces left. Add the flour mixture and use a fork to blend until a dough forms. Gather the dough and knead until smooth. Roll the dough into a 6-inch log, wrap in plastic, and refrigerate until chilled, at least 2 hours.

Use scissors to cut the fruit into halves or quarters to cook more quickly. In a medium saucepan, combine the fruit with the water and bring to a boil. Cover and cook over low heat, stirring occasionally and adding water as needed. Cook until fruit is very soft and the liquid has been absorbed, about 45 minutes. Remove from heat. Mash a bit with a potato masher, then add ⅓ cup of the sorghum and mash together until fully blended. Taste and add more sorghum, if desired, stirring to incorporate it fully. Allow to cool to room temperature. (This can be refrigerated until you are ready to fry the pies but bring back to room temperature before you do.)

Cut the log of dough into 12 even pieces and roll each piece into a ball. Working with half of the balls at a time, on a very lightly floured surface, roll out each ball to a 6-inch round. Brush the edges with water. Mound 2 heaping tablespoons of the apple filling on the lower half of each round. Fold the dough over the filling to make a half-moon, leaving a ½-inch border; press the edges to seal. Using a lightly floured fork, crimp the edges decoratively. Transfer the pies to a large, lightly floured baking sheet and repeat with the remaining balls of dough and filling. Note that you want to be sure to seal the pies well so no filling slips into the hot grease, which would cause it to pop and splatter. I use a bit of cold water on my finger to secure the seal, making sure it dries before frying.

In a wide, heavy skillet, heat enough lard to make a pool about ½-inch deep on medium-high. When it's hot enough that a tiny pinch of dough dropped in dances and turns golden, lay a few pies into the skillet very carefully (I use a metal spatula, but my aunt Minnie could do this barehanded and never burned a finger). Make sure not to crowd the skillet, but fry pies in small batches, turning once when the first side turns golden and continuing until the second does. Remove and drain on a rack above paper towels. Allow to cool a bit, but serve while warm. Makes 1 dozen.

Berry Shortcakes with Sorghum Crème Fraîche

Ouita Michel loves to make the most of the products and traditions of the bluegrass region. Baking quick, sweetened biscuits to soak up the juicy bounty of local berries has long been how central Kentuckians say shortcake. A little sorghum just adds a tang of sweetness to the drawl.

This recipe comes in three parts to be assembled when you want to serve. You need to prepare the crème fraîche the day before and to begin Ouita's Biscuits, which need to chill before baking, at least an hour before you wish to serve. Macerate the berries while the biscuits are baking.

CRÈME FRAÎCHE

½ cup sour cream
1 cup heavy cream
3 tablespoons sorghum syrup, gently warmed until pourable
½ teaspoon vanilla

Whisk sour cream in a small mixing bowl and slowly whisk in heavy cream. Cover bowl with cheesecloth and let sit in a warm spot for 12 to 18 hours.

Uncover, whisk, and transfer to a glass or plastic container. Chill. Just before you are ready to use, whisk in sorghum and vanilla.

OUITA'S BISCUITS

Follow instructions for Ouita's Biscuits on page 63. Allow biscuits to cool, and slice horizontally in three sections.

MACERATED BERRIES

---

2 cups mixed berries, such as raspberries, sliced strawberries,
    blueberries, or currants
2 tablespoons sugar
Splash of liqueur, such as Grand Marnier

Macerate mixed berries with sugar and liqueur. Allow to sit for 20
minutes.

To assemble, gently spoon berries and their juices, topped with
sorghum crème fraîche, between layers of each biscuit. Top with
more crème fraîche and a drizzle of remaining fruit juices for color.
Makes 12.

Black Walnut Angel Food Cake with Sorghum Syrup

Angel food, indeed. I like to imagine that James Beard Award–winning
pastry chef Karen Barker's inspired rendition is what the saints serve in
Tex Ritter's "Hillbilly Heaven." If so, it would be a cake to die for. But
you don't have to go that far to taste this divinity. Just use the recipe
here, reprinted from *Sweet Stuff: Karen Barker's American Desserts*.

Black walnuts are not the same as ubiquitous English walnuts. Like
sorghum compared to honey, black walnuts have a deeper, more intense
flavor, reminiscent of liqueur. They are worth seeking out, and in the
fall, you may find them in the same farmers markets, country stores,
and online sources where you can find sweet sorghum syrup. At least
one major nut distributor also sells them, packaged, from groceries.

---

1 cup lightly toasted, finely chopped black walnuts
½ teaspoon cinnamon
1 cup plus 2 tablespoons cake flour
1½ cups sugar, divided
¼ teaspoon kosher salt
1¾ cups egg whites (about 12 to 14), at room temperature
    (see note)

1½ teaspoons cream of tartar

3 tablespoons sorghum syrup

1 teaspoon vanilla

Heat oven to 350°F.

In a small bowl, combine the walnuts with cinnamon and set aside.

Triple sift the flour with ½ cup of the sugar. Add the salt and set aside.

Using a mixer with a whip attachment, beat the egg whites till foamy. Add the cream of tartar and beat until soft peaks just start to form. Gradually add the remaining 1 cup of sugar, ¼ cup at a time, and beat till medium peaks form. Transfer the beaten whites to a large mixing bowl.

In 3 additions, sprinkle the reserved flour mixture over the whites and delicately but thoroughly fold to combine. Fold in the sorghum and vanilla.

Place ⅓ of the batter in a 10-inch tube pan with a removable bottom (but not a nonstick pan). Sprinkle with ½ of the reserved walnut mixture. Top with another ⅓ of the batter, spreading lightly with a small offset spatula if necessary. Sprinkle with the remaining walnuts and top with the remaining batter.

Bake for 35 to 40 minutes, until the cake is golden brown and springy to the touch. Remove from oven and immediately invert. If your pan has little "feet" on the bottom, you can simply turn the pan upside down to cool. If not, hang the inverted pan over a narrow-necked wine bottle or a large funnel to cool. Allow to cool completely (2 to 3 hours).

To remove the cake from the pan, run a long thin-bladed knife around the outer perimeter of the pan to loosen the sides. Push up on the removable bottom to remove the cake. Loosen the cake from the center of the tube by again inserting a thin-bladed knife and tracing around the tube. Loosen the bottom of the cake as well. Turn the cake out onto a parchment-paper-lined baking sheet. Cover with a service platter and reinvert so that the cake is right side up. To serve, slice with a serrated knife. This cake should be served the day it's made.

Note: Packaged pasteurized egg whites in the cooler of the grocery and powdered egg whites can be handy in some cases, but they cannot be substituted for the real deal, fresh from the egg, when baking, particularly when baking an angel food cake. This is not an abstract aesthetic point: They simply won't perform the same way and the dense, flat result will seem more like food from purgatory than a heavenly delight.

So what to do with those extra egg yolks? There are plenty of recipes that call for yolks alone, and they are also a wonderful enrichment added to the whole egg mixture for scrambled eggs or French toast. You can freeze them individually to keep them until you need them. Have a clean ice cube tray on hand as you separate the eggs and plop a yolk into each compartment as you go. Before you place them in the freezer, use a fork to pierce and stir a bit. Freeze solid, and then you can remove them from the tray and transfer them to a plastic freezer bag to use later. Remove as needed and allow to defrost to liquid state before using in a recipe.

Audrey Morgan's Apple-Sorghum Stack Cake

Chef Sean Brock's Husk (in Nashville, Tennessee, and Charleston, South Carolina) and McCrady's (also Charleston) are celebrated for their new riffs on southern cuisine, particularly that of the low country. But underpinning all of his explorations into new foodways is a passion for the foodways of his homeplace in the southern highlands of southwest Virginia. There, he recalled, "each year we had a sorghum potluck" where family and neighbors would come together to boil the syrup. "The beauty is how it brings a community together," he said. "When you lose the sorghum, it's just another thing we lose as a culture."

To keep from losing that, Sean shared his grandmother Audrey's rendition of an Appalachian Mountain stack cake. Sean's version calls for canola oil, but he said his grandmother used shortening when she made it, and he notes that good lard would be delicious. Sean's kitchens have the six 10-inch springform pans needed to bake all the layers simultaneously. If yours doesn't, you can bake layers one at a time, the way it was traditionally done in the mountains.

APPLE BUTTER

12 cups chopped, unpeeled apples, preferably Pippin or Granny Smith

¾ cup apple cider

1 cup sugar

2 teaspoons ground ginger

1 teaspoon ground cinnamon

1 teaspoon nutmeg

½ teaspoon ground cloves

CAKE

9 cups self-rising flour

2 cups sugar

4 teaspoons ground ginger

2 teaspoons allspice

2 teaspoons cinnamon

1½ cups canola oil

2 cups buttermilk

2 cups sorghum syrup

6 eggs, lightly beaten

GLAZE

2 cups brown sugar

½ cup rye whiskey or bourbon

14 ounces sweetened condensed milk

¼ pound (1 stick) unsalted butter, diced

½ cup milk

1 teaspoon pure vanilla extract

For the apple butter: Combine the apples and cider in a nonreactive heavy-bottomed 3-quart pot. Cover the pot and cook the apples on low heat, stirring occasionally, until the apples are soft, about 8 hours. Purée the apples in a food sieve or food mill. Return the puréed apples to the pot. Add the sugar and spices, cover, and cook on low heat, stirring frequently to prevent scorching, until it is very thick, 1 to 2 hours. You want it to be a spread with no excess moisture. Makes 9 cups.

Put the apple butter in a container, cool to room temperature, cover, and refrigerate. Tightly covered, the apple butter will keep for several weeks in the refrigerator or it may be frozen for up to 3 months.

For the cake: Preheat oven to 350°F. You will need to make 6 cake layers, each of which will be divided in half. This is easiest to do if you have 6 (10-inch) springform pans. Cut 6 circles of parchment paper the size of the bottom of a 10-inch springform pan. Prepare the 6 pans by greasing the bottom and sides with butter. Lay a parchment circle in the bottom of each and grease with butter.

Sift the flour, sugar, ginger, allspice, and cinnamon into a large mixing bowl and combine well.

In a separate large bowl, gently whisk the oil, buttermilk, and sorghum into the eggs. You do not want to make a lot of froth.

Slowly stir the wet mixture into the dry mixture. Pour ½ inch of batter into each of the 6 prepared pans. Bake for 10 minutes, until a toothpick comes out dry. Allow the layers to cool in the pans on baking racks on the countertop for 1 hour.

Unlock the springform pans and remove the cake layers from the pans. Using a long, serrated knife, carefully split each layer in half, as follows. Make 4 evenly spaced horizontal marks with your knife around the layer halfway up the side. Slice a few inches in toward the center at each mark. Turn the layer and slice in a little more at each mark. You want the 4 cuts to meet at the center, but it's best to go carefully so that you get 2 even layers. Once you have sliced through to the center, put a hand on the top of the layer and use your knife with the other hand to help you lift off the top layer. Repeat with the remaining 5 layers to make a total of 12 split layers.

Place 1 split layer of the cake cut-side up on a cake plate. Evenly spread 6 ounces of room-temperature apple butter on it. Place a cake layer cut-side down on top of the apple butter. Evenly spread 6 ounces of apple butter on top of it. Continue the process with the remaining layers of cake. The last layer should be cut-side down and should not have apple butter spread on it.

For the glaze: Combine the brown sugar, whiskey, and condensed milk in a medium saucepan over medium heat and cook the mixture, stirring constantly, until the sugar dissolves, about 7 minutes. Remove the saucepan from the heat and stir in the butter. When it is incorporated, stir in the milk and the vanilla extract. Cool on the countertop for 7 minutes before glazing.

Carefully pour the glaze over the top of the cake, allowing it to run down over the sides. Using a cake spatula, spread the glaze evenly over the outside of the cake.

Put the cake in a cake keeper or cake box and let the cake set out overnight before cutting. Covered, the cake will keep for up to 3 days at room temperature and 5 days in the refrigerator.

Woodford Pudding with Sorghum Caramel Sauce

Like a quick and easy jam cake is how Chef Ouita Michel describes this pudding, which has been made by the cooks in Woodford County, Kentucky, since before the Civil War. Like heaven would be my take. You serve the warm pudding topped with Sorghum Caramel Sauce, and to keep with the regional theme, I'd suggest you make it with a bit of good bourbon. Woodford Reserve would be appropriate.

1 cup flour
1 teaspoon cinnamon
½ teaspoon mace
½ teaspoon ground cardamom
¼ teaspoon salt
1 cup brown sugar
¼ pound (1 stick) butter
3 eggs
1 teaspoon baking soda
½ cup buttermilk
1 cup blackberry jam
Sorghum Caramel Sauce (page 57)

Heat oven to 350°F. Grease a 9-inch square baking pan or cake pan and set aside.

Sift flour with spices and salt and set aside.

In a large bowl cream sugar with butter, then add the eggs, one at a time, beating to incorporate after each. Dissolve baking soda in buttermilk and add. Add flour mixture and mix until well blended, then add the jam. When batter is well blended, pour into greased pan and bake for 40 minutes, or until the center feels light and spongy.

Serve warm with about 1 tablespoon of room-temperature Sorghum Caramel Sauce spooned on each serving. Pass extra sauce. Serves 6 to 8.

Sorghum Ginger Snaps

Sorghum and ginger is a classic pairing and they make a classic cookie. For extra oomph, you can add candied ginger.

¾ cup lard or shortening

1 cup sugar, plus extra for rolling

1 egg

⅓ cup sorghum syrup

2 cups flour

1½ teaspoons baking soda

½ teaspoon salt

1 teaspoon ginger

1 teaspoon cinnamon

¾ cup finely chopped candied ginger (optional)

Beat shortening and sugar to blend, then beat in egg and sorghum. Add remaining ingredients except extra sugar and beat to blend. Cover and refrigerate an hour or more.

Heat oven to 350°F. Form into 1½-inch balls and roll in sugar. Place 2 inches apart on a cookie sheet. Bake 10 to 12 minutes for soft cookies, a minute longer for snaps. Makes about 3 dozen.

Fig and Cranberry Cookies

Autumnal treats for the tummy, these plump little cookies are chock full of goodness.

---

6 to 8 whole figs
½ cup dried cranberries
¼ pound (1 stick) butter, softened
½ cup sugar
1 cup sorghum syrup
1 egg
3 cups flour
1 teaspoon baking powder
1 teaspoon baking soda
1 teaspoon allspice
1 teaspoon ground cinnamon
½ teaspoon salt

Heat oven to 350°F.

Cut figs into pieces similar in size to the dried cranberries. You want ¾ cup. Mix with cranberries and set aside.

In a large bowl, cream together the butter, sugar, and sorghum. Add the egg and blend.

Sift together the flour and remaining ingredients. Add to the wet ingredients in 3 increments, stirring after each. Stir in the dried fruit.

Use a tablespoon measure to scoop out generously mounded dollops of dough on a cookie sheet, leaving 2 inches between. Bake for 12 minutes, or until solid on top and lightly browned on the edges. Transfer to rack and allow to cool. Makes about 2 dozen.

Gone, Gone, Gone Peanut-Butter Cookies

It's true, I could have gone all Elvis and studded these with bacon and banana, but why mess with the perfect pair of smooth organic peanut butter and rich amber sorghum? They harmonize just like Phil and Don. Want to know what I mean? Check out the Everly Brothers singing their hit "Gone, Gone, Gone" on YouTube while you wait for these babies to bake and cool. You'll be grinning by the time you pour yourself a glass of cold milk.

1 tablespoon butter, softened
⅓ cup creamy peanut butter
⅓ cup sugar
¼ cup sorghum syrup
1 egg
1 teaspoon vanilla
1 cup flour
½ teaspoon baking soda
½ teaspoon baking powder
¼ teaspoon salt

Heat oven to 375°F.

In a large bowl, cream butter and peanut butter. Add sugar and cream to combine; add sorghum and do the same. Add egg and vanilla and mix well.

Sift together dry ingredients and incorporate into peanut butter mixture ⅓ cup at a time. You may want to lightly knead the dough to combine at the last. Form dough into spheres about the size of a Ping-Pong ball and place about 2 inches apart on cookie sheet. Lightly press down on top with the tines of a fork. Bake for 8 to 10 minutes, removing when tops are firm and bottom has just barely started to turn. Cool for 5 minutes on pan before removing to rack to finish cooling. Makes about 18 cookies.

Masala Mama Cookies

Sweet spice with just a little bite makes this a seductively interesting cookie. Pair with Mango Sorghum Ice Cream (page 150).

¼ pound plus 4 tablespoons (1½ sticks) butter, softened
½ cup sugar
1 egg
¼ cup sorghum syrup
2¼ cups flour
2 teaspoons baking soda
2 teaspoons ginger
1 teaspoon ground cloves
¾ teaspoon ground cinnamon
¼ teaspoon salt

Heat oven to 350°F.

In a large bowl, cream together butter and sugar. Add egg and sorghum and beat until well blended.

Sift together remaining ingredients and add to the wet mixture in thirds, mixing to incorporate after each addition. Form into 2-inch balls and place on cookie sheet 2 inches apart. Bake for 13 to 15 minutes. Makes about 2 dozen.

Long Sweetening Sorbet

At John Fleer's Rhubarb in Asheville, this sorbet comes on a pretty plate with lots of trimmings, including fried apples. If you want to try that combo, there's a recipe on page 95. But I'm here to tell you this crisply delightful treat can stand just fine on its own. You may increase proportions to suit your ice cream maker.

2 cups apple cider
⅓ cup plus 1 tablespoon sorghum syrup
½ cinnamon stick
½ vanilla bean, split
¼ cup buttermilk, plus more if needed
1 egg, whole with intact shell
Anna's Sorghum Simple Syrup (page 122), if needed

In a saucepan, over medium heat, combine cider, sorghum, cinnamon, and vanilla and simmer for 5 minutes, gently stirring until sorghum is dissolved. Remove from heat and allow to cool slightly.

Temper the buttermilk by drizzling small amounts of the cider mixture into it while whisking. Continue until the two liquids are combined. Test with egg (see note), and when the mixture passes the test, process in ice cream maker according to manufacturer instructions.

Note: For a sorbet to have the proper consistency it must have sufficient sugar in the mix. You can test for this using an instrument called a refractor, or by using an egg. Wash the egg, rinse, and dry, then gently place it in the sorbet mix. It should sink, but only so far that an area about the size of a quarter remains exposed on top. If it sinks all the way, or if the area is smaller—say, dime size—you need to add more sweetening. Remove the egg and rinse. Add a tablespoon of simple syrup and test again. If too much of the egg remains exposed, add a little more buttermilk.

Mango Sorghum Ice Cream

The trick to this recipe is allowing the mixture to cure for at least 8 hours in the refrigerator before making the ice cream, and then in the freezer for 2 hours after, so start early in the day for supper, or the night before. Pair this decadent ice cream with Masala Mama Cookies (page 148). You won't need much to be satisfied!

2 ripe mangoes
Zest and juice of 1 lime
½ cup sugar
1 tablespoon sorghum syrup
Dash of salt
2 cups heavy cream

Peel and pit the mangoes and chop the flesh coarsely. Process in a blender or food processor to make a smooth purée. Add the lime zest and juice, sugar, sorghum, and salt. Process again to dissolve the sugar, about a minute. Scrape the purée into a bowl and whisk in the cream. Cover and refrigerate for at least 8 hours.

Freeze the mango cream mixture according to the instructions for your ice cream maker. Transfer to a container with a lid, and let the ice cream cure in the freezer for at least 2 hours before serving. Makes about 4 cups.

Sorghum and Grits Ice Cream

Shortly after word got out that I was working on a cookbook about sorghum syrup, friends in Louisville, Kentucky, began to contact me. "Have you tasted Chef Edward Lee's sorghum and grits ice cream?" they asked. Or, more often, "Can you get that recipe?" Indeed, the answers are "Yes, wow!" and "Yes indeed!" Here's the recipe for this soon-to-be-classic dessert from Edward Lee's newest Louisville venue, MilkWood.

1½ cups milk

1½ cups heavy cream

¾ cup sorghum syrup, plus more for drizzling

1 tablespoon light brown sugar

1 large egg

1 egg yolk

Pinch of sea salt

⅓ cup of cooked grits, dried and separated

In a saucepan over medium-low heat, bring milk, cream, sorghum, and brown sugar to a gentle simmer, stirring until the cream mixture is smooth.

In a separate bowl, whisk together the egg and the yolk with the pinch of salt. Slowly add the warm cream mixture to the egg mixture until combined. Pour custard through a fine mesh sieve and then cool in the fridge for a couple of hours.

Churn in an ice cream maker, and right before it is done, slowly add the grits a little at a time until all are mixed into the ice cream.

Transfer ice cream to a container and freeze for at least 1 hour. When ready to eat, let the ice cream sit out for about 15 minutes before serving. Serve with a little more sorghum drizzled over the top. Serves 6.

Note: Drizzled sorghum syrup is a wonderful way to jazz up store-bought ice cream. Chocolate, coffee, peach, and vanilla all pair nicely, but my absolute favorite is black walnut.

Resources

Books

The twelve volumes in the Foxfire series contain numerous references to sorghum and molasses, but of particular note is the twelve-page illustrated section on sorghum making in *Foxfire 3* (Anchor Press, 1975).

Jean Ritchie's *Singing Family of the Cumberlands* (University Press of Kentucky, 1988) is an evocative memoir of growing up in the southern Appalachians in the early twentieth century, including a memorable sorghum squeezing.

Rona Roberts's *Sweet, Sweet Sorghum: Kentucky's Golden Wonder* (Hotcakes Press, 2011) is a celebration of that state's sweet sorghum traditions and burgeoning industry.

David Shields's *Southern Provisions: On the Creation and Resuscitation of Regional Cuisine* (University of Chicago Press, 2015) contains a chapter on sorghum that gives a detailed historical account of sweet sorghum syrups' arrival and progress in the United States.

Videos

Fred Sauceman and East Tennessee State University are producing a video on the Guenthers of Muddy Pond and other sorghum processors in the central and east Tennessee regions. For more information, or to order the video, contact:

Fred Sauceman
East Tennessee State University
Box 70717
Johnson City, TN 37614
423-439-4317
sauceman@etsu.edu.

Acknowledgments

With thanks to Meghan, Todd, and Finn, for bringing me home and making it easy to stay.

With thanks to Lisa Ekus and Sian Hunter, who saw the light and let it shine.

With gratitude to everyone who gave so generously to this project, some named herein, some not.

And most especially to John Stehling, who came along for the ride, and Julie, who let him.

Photography Credits

Photos by John Rott appear on pages ii, 54, 62, 74, 84, 98, 118, and 130.

Photos by Fred Sauceman at Muddy Pond Sorghum Mill in Monterey, Tennessee, appear on pages 7, 20, 22, 23, and 25.

Photos by John Stehling at Hughes' Sorghum in Young Harris, Georgia, appear on pages 24 and 49.

Index

RONNI LUNDY has been a frequent contributor to *Food & Wine*, *Gourmet*, and *Esquire*. She is the author of eight books, including *Shuck Beans, Stack Cakes, and Honest Fried Chicken* and *Cornbread Nation 3: Foods of the Mountain South*.